RICHARD CURTIS

Four Appendices and a Screenplay

CORGI BOOKS

FOUR WEDDINGS AND A FUNERAL
A CORGI BOOK: 0552143294

First Publication in Great Britain.

PRINTING HISTORY

Corgi edition published 1994.

Publication of this screenplay by kind permission of
Richard Curtis.

Additional material © Richard Curtis 1994.

CORGI BOOKS ARE PUBLISHED BY

TRANSWORLD PUBLISHERS LTD
61-63 Uxbridge Road, Ealing, London W5 5SA.

TRANSWORLD PUBLISHERS (AUSTRALIA) PTY LTD
15-25 Helles Avenue, Moorebank, NSW 2170.

TRANSWORLD PUBLISHERS (NZ) LTD
3 William Pickering Drive, Albany, Auckland.

Photographs by Stephen Morley, reprinted by kind
permission of Polygram Filmed Entertainment © Polygram
Filmed Entertainment 1994.

The text of 'Funeral Blues' by W.H. Auden (*Another Time*,
1940) is reprinted from *Collected Poems* edited by Edward
Mendelson, by permission of Faber and Faber Ltd on behalf
of the Auden Estate.

Can't Smile Without You, written by Chris Arnold, David
Martin and Geoff Morrow © 1975 Dick James Music Ltd.
Lyrics reproduced by kind permission of the publishers.

Book design by Julia Lloyd.

Printed and bound in Great Britain
by Jarrold & Sons Ltd, Norwich.

FOUR DEDICATIONS

To Mike, Duncan and all the team and crew,
who made a silk purse.

To all the actors in the film, who fleshed out my
stick people.

To my Gran, who taught me to roar with
laughter when I was 5, and saw this film and
still laughed at the age of 90.

To Emma.

AND AN APOLOGY

To all my friends whose weddings I went to,
forgot to buy presents for and then shamelessly
nicked incidents from.

A WORKING TITLE PRODUCTION

A **MIKE NEWELL** Film

HUGH GRANT ANDIE MACDOWELL

four Weddings and a funeral

KRISTIN SCOTT THOMAS SIMON CALLOW

JAMES FLEET CHARLOTTE COLEMAN

JOHN HANNAH DAVID BOWER

CORIN REDGRAVE & ROWAN ATKINSON

Casting Director **MICHELLE GUISH**

U.S. Casting **DAVID RUBIN**

Production Designer **MAGGIE GRAY**

Costume Designer **LINDY HEMMING**

Editor **JON GREGORY**

Director of Photography **MICHAEL COULTER B.S.C.**

Original Music by **RICHARD RODNEY BENNETT**

Co-Executive Producer **RICHARD CURTIS**

Executive Producers **TIM BEVAN** & **ERIC FELLNER**

Written by **RICHARD CURTIS**

Produced by **DUNCAN KENWORTHY**

Directed by **MIKE NEWELL**

PolyGram
Filmed Entertainment

Contents

Introduction

I feel sheepish about writing an actual introduction – so here is an article I wrote for the Observer in the week the film came out, which says some of the things an introduction might have said.

FOUR RULES AND A SUGGESTION

Everyone who ever wrote a film hates Sylvester Stallone most of all. Apparently, he locked himself in a room for three days and wrote 'Rocky', the first one, which is a marvellous script and an excellent movie. But mostly things don't happen that way. Writing a film script is a stupidly long process, and for everyone except Sylvester, a pretty agonising one.

Three years ago I started writing a film called 'Four Weddings and A Funeral' which comes out this Friday. I'm sure my experiences with it can't be generalised about – but just in case there are any prospective screenwriters amongst you, here is my simplistic stab at Four Rules and a Suggestion for screen-writing.

My first rule is that you let things stew. I've twice written films straight after I thought up the idea and they were both disastrous. In 1989 I thought of an idea for a film about dreams, complete, at a petrol station on the A40. I drove home and started writing frantically. Six weeks later it was finished. Six weeks and one day later it was in the dustbin. I re-read it, and I realised it was well-constructed twaddle, it meant absolutely nothing to me. On the other occasion, I wrote a film for America, to please Americans, which I made up on the way to a 'pitch-meeting'. Two whole years of writing later, I attended another meeting at MGM – they told me they absolutely loved the film, provided I could change the character of the leading man, the second lead, the cameos, the dialogue and the jokes. I said that only left the title. They said they wanted to change the title too. So that's the first thing – it helps to let things stew in your head a while to find out if you really care. The process of film-making is SO DETAILED and SO LONG, nothing fraudulent is going to escape discovery.

My second rule is – try not to pitch: if you can avoid it, try not to get commissioned. Now this is a tough one, because most of us need the money – but the problem with pitching things, and with treatments is that two people can read the same bit of paper and sit in the same room having the same discussion, but they never hear the same thing. One of them leaves intending to writing biting social satire – the other happily describes how he's commissioned a sexy pants-and-knickers farce. Then, as the writer writes, the film comes to life, and changes. It's no longer a social satire, it's a dead serious state-of-the-nation film, moved from the original Westminster location to the brooding Shetland Islands. So you deliver your film, and the man who commissioned it is INEVITABLY disappointed. The next year is spent reconciling a film now called 'Earthwomb' with the original treatment, called 'Sir Peter's Trousers'. So if you can write the thing first, at least the people who buy it, if they buy it, are under no misapprehension what they're paying for.

On to rule three. If you possibly can, get your work edited by someone you love. My first film, called 'The Tall Guy', was a four hour muddle before my best friend Helen got her hands on it. Five different times she read it and cut it down. The film that was accepted was the fifth draft by me and her. 'Four Weddings' is a co-operation between me and my girl Emma. She read every draft of every scene from the beginning of the process to the end. For a year I lived in terror of the fatal initials 'C.D.B.' scattered through everything she read. 'C.D.B.' stands for 'Could Do Better'. Once again, you're lucky if you can get this – but the thing about a friend, girlfriend, boyfriend, wife or husband is that they understand what you're getting at. They have no hidden agenda – they want the film to be good, and to be your film – not just profitable and a perfect vehicle for John Thaw.

Rule Four is – don't count the rewrites or it will drive you mad. These were the rewrites on 'Four Weddings' – five for Emma before it was ever handed in. One after talking to Duncan, my producer and Debra at Working Title, the production company. Then two big ones for Mike Newell, the director, and Duncan, as we tried to give every character proper stories, rather than just jokes. Then there was one after the first round of casting: actors reading the lines tend to show just clunky the script is! The next rewrite came after Channel 4 expressed worries about it all being a bit 'smart'. Then the film was delayed for six months, so there was one long rewrite to fill the time and to try to crack the really knotty problems with the end. At one point, Emma and I escaped to Europe, and spent a month on one 2 minute scene. Then there was another rewrite during the second round of casting. Then one when our budget went from £3.5 million to £3.2. Then another one when it went from £3.2 to £2.7, which consisted of cutting down the cast: 'a' vicar, became 'the vicar you saw earlier'. After the read-through (when no one laughed at 15% of the 'jokes' and DID laugh at 25% of the serious bits), there was another hefty hack. During rehearsals another. That's seventeen, and I've got a nasty feeling I've forgotten one or two. And the horrible thing about this rule is part two of it – don't resent the rewrites – the awful painful truth is that the script probably did get a bit better each time.

And so on to the suggestion. **I suggest that** – after you have let an idea stew, written the film you wanted without the compromises of a commission, let it be brutally edited by someone you love and then re-written it fifteen times – **you cast Hugh Grant as the lead.** It doesn't matter what the character is – if she's a middle-aged cop on the verge of retiring, Hugh will be perfect. If he's an Eskimo schoolboy – Hugh is exactly what you are looking for. This weekend 'Four Weddings and a Funeral' may pass the thirty million dollar mark in America, and relatives in New York tell me that's really down to Hugh. If only we'd been canny, and cast him in the Andie MacDowell, Simon Callow and Rowan Atkinson roles as well, it could have been fifty million by now. And that's the hell of it. Whatever your script is like, no matter how much stewing and rewriting – if the punters don't want to sleep with the star, you may never be asked to write another one.

Wedding 1

MAY 1ST

1. INT. CHARLES'S BEDROOM. CHARLES & SCARLETT'S HOUSE. LONDON. DAY.

The bedroom is white, and full of clutter. At ground level, clothes are thrown about on a minimum of furniture. CHARLES is asleep. His alarm clock goes off. His hand sweeps up, and switches it off. He stays asleep. Gershwin's 'But Not For Me', sung by Elton John, plays.

2. INT. TOM'S BEDROOM. TOM & FIONA'S HOUSE. LONDON. DAY.

Another alarm clock is ringing. TOM sits bolt upright in his pyjamas. He is a very high-spirited, very affectionate and very stupid aristocrat. He leaps out of bed, opens a little case and takes out a tailcoat.

3. INT. FIONA'S BEDROOM. TOM & FIONA'S HOUSE. DAY.

FIONA is tall, attractive, intelligent, aristocratic, 33. TOM's sister and his utter opposite. She holds up two dresses – she puts one in front of her and looks in the mirror – pulls a disapproving face – then holds up the other – pulls a face at that too – she doesn't like either of them.

4. INT. KITCHEN. MATTHEW & GARETH'S HOUSE. LONDON. DAY.

GARETH *is cooking a full English breakfast. He is about 45 – overweight, bearded, with rosy cheeks and disposition. Behind him,* MATTHEW *puts on a tie. He is 33, clean shaven, intelligent, with a very kind face. As* GARETH *brings over the breakfast,* MATTHEW *wipes a little shaving foam off his cheek.*

5. INT. CHARLES'S BEDROOM. CHARLES & SCARLETT'S HOUSE. DAY.

CHARLES *is still fast asleep.*

6. INT. FIONA'S BEDROOM. TOM & FIONA'S HOUSE. DAY.

FIONA *glides downstairs in the very elegant house she shares with* TOM. TOM *is hungrily eating breakfast. She takes a sip of coffee, and then moves to leave.* TOM *rushes after her with toast in his mouth.*

7. EXT. MATTHEW & GARETH'S HOUSE. DAY.

FIONA *and* TOM *pull up in Tom's Land Rover outside a charming small mews house, where* MATTHEW *and* GARETH *are waiting for them. It looks like a little country cottage, but in the middle of London.* GARETH *points to his watch, implying they're just a little late. He now wears a luscious waistcoat portraying two naked golden cherubs, kissing across the buttons.*

Now DAVID *walks coolly down the street towards them: he's about 30, slender, self-possessed.*

8. EXT. THE EMBANKMENT. DAY.

The Land Rover drives along beside the Thames, at high speed.

9. INT. CHARLES'S BEDROOM. CHARLES & SCARLETT'S HOUSE. DAY.

CHARLES *is still asleep.*

10. EXT. MOTORWAY. DAY.

TOM *and* FIONA*'s Land Rover calmly proceeds along the motorway.*

11. INT. CHARLES'S BEDROOM. CHARLES & SCARLETT'S HOUSE. DAY.

CHARLES *turns, and wakes. He reaches over sleepily, grabs his alarm clock and looks at it.*

    CHARLES: **O, fuck.**

CHARLES *is 33, fairly good-looking, fairly ironic.*

12. INT. SCARLETT'S BEDROOM. CHARLES & SCARLETT'S HOUSE. DAY.

If you thought CHARLES*'s room was untidy, you hadn't seen this one. It is a massive mess, with startlingly miscellaneous clothing everywhere.* CHARLES*'s friend,* SCARLETT, *25, lives there.* CHARLES *taps her on the shoulder: she is deeply asleep, and, when woken, confused.*

He picks up her alarm, which is red and by the bed, and shows it to her. She peeks through sleepy eyes. She's not at all upper class.

    SCARLETT: **O fuck.**

13. INT. CHARLES'S BEDROOM. CHARLES & SCARLETT'S HOUSE. DAY.

Close-up of CHARLES's *fingers connecting his braces to the back of his wedding trousers. He bends to tie his shoes, and the braces ping off the back of the trousers.*

Charles: Fuck.

14. EXT. CHARLES'S CAR. DAY.

CHARLES *and* SCARLETT *are sitting in a seedy looking old Volvo. The engine chortles horribly – it won't start.*

CHARLES: Fuck. Right – we take yours.

SCARLETT: It only goes forty miles an hour.

15. EXT. MOTORWAY. DAY.

SCARLETT's *tiny Mini Cooper 'S' is speeding along the motorway at a tremendously illegal speed – definitely twice 40 miles an hour. It is shaking with the effort.*

16. INT/EXT. SCARLETT'S CAR. MOTORWAY. DAY.

CHARLES: What turn-off?

SCARLETT *faffs a little, picking up the map for the first time. They shoot past an exit sign.*

CHARLES: It'd better not be the B359.

She finds it proudly.

SCARLETT: It's the B359.

CHARLES: Fuck it.

He jams on the brake. Reverses 50 yards back up the motorway.

SCARLETT: Fuck.

They almost die, then shoot up the sliproad of the B359.

CHARLES: Fuck.

17. EXT. WEDDING 1. COUNTRY CHURCH. DAY.

An idyllic sun-soaked small country church, in Somerset. The Mini screeches up, jams on the brakes and skids into a lay-by 100 yards away. CHARLES *and* SCARLETT *leap out of the car, and dress in their formal gear.*

CHARLES: Fuck.

SCARLETT: Fuck, fuck.

He zips up the back of her dress and it catches.

Charles: Fuck, fuckity fuck.

She straightens his tie. Over her shoulder, a large Rolls Royce appears and shoots past them. It is the bridal car. They look at each other. Tiny pause.

Charles: Bugger.

They sprint towards the church.

The bride is just getting out of the car. CHARLES *and* SCARLETT *whip past, with a smile and a friendly wave.*

You are cordially
invited to attend the wedding of

Angus & Laura

St. John's Church, Stoke Clandon,
Somerset, England

18. INT. WEDDING 1. COUNTRY CHURCH. DAY.

The church is glowing white, and be-decked with flowers. CHARLES *and* SCARLETT *survey the weddingly scene of hats and flowers. Their eyes fall upon their friends. They head for them.*

FIONA: **There's a sort of greatness to your lateness.**

CHARLES: **Thanks. It's not achieved without real suffering.**

SCARLETT *slips in –* CHARLES *acknowledges them all with a wave and heads on quickly up the aisle to where the groom is standing. His name is* ANGUS *and he's a little tense.*

CHARLES: **I'm so, so sorry, Angus. Inexcusable. I'll be killing myself after the service, if it's any consolation.**

ANGUS: **Doesn't matter – Tom was standing by...**

CHARLES: Thanks, Tom. You're a saint. And...disastrous haircut.

TOM *gives an enthusiastic thumbs up and heads back down to join the friends.*

ANGUS: As long as you haven't forgotten the rings.

CHARLES: Nope.

He pats his pocket confidently. When ANGUS *looks away we see a look of concern slip over* CHARLES's *face – he has just patted an empty pocket.*

At that moment, a girl with a large black hat walks in, and down the aisle. She vaguely uses the hat to shield her against curious eyes.

CHARLES: Tssk. I hate people being late. Hate it.

ANGUS *appreciates the effort to relax him and gives* CHARLES *a half smile. And at that moment the wedding march starts.*

CHARLES: Here we go...

ANGUS *turns to look down the aisle at his bride.*

CUT TO: *The bride,* LAURA, *on the arm of her father, with two little and one fully-grown bridesmaid,* LYDIA. LAURA *looks a little over-fulsome – the row of friends turns as she passes.*

> SCARLETT: O, isn't she lovely!!

> FIONA: Scarlett, you're blind. She looks like a big meringue.

The bride reaches the front and the VICAR *starts the service.*

> VICAR: Dear friends – what a joy it is to welcome you to our church on this wonderful day for Angus and Laura.

CHARLES *looks around behind him, trying to find a way out of his dilemma. His eyes land on the girl in the black hat. Then he remembers: he's got a more important immediate problem. He checks his waistcoat pocket – still no ring.*

> VICAR: Before we start the service, let us all join together in the first hymn.

They stand – there is a slight wobble on the organ, and a grinding up to tempo as we hear the intro to 'Jerusalem'.

CUT INTO: *The singing.* CHARLES *is trying to attract the attention of his friends, all in their row. Finally* MATTHEW *sees him and* CHARLES *manages to mime the problem.* MATTHEW *smacks his head in mock despair.* CHARLES *does a little plea. He needs help.*

MATTHEW *whispers something in* GARETH's *ear.* GARETH *holds out his hands to reveal no ring. He in turn whispers to* FIONA.

Cut through four pairs of ring-less hands. MATTHEW *asks* TOM. *Nothing. Finally...*

MATTHEW: *(Loud whispering)* **Scarlett?**

She gives him a big innocent 'What?' smile she is the last resort.

TIME CUT ON TO:

> **VICAR:** Dearly beloved – we are gathered together here in the sight of God and in the face of this congregation to join together this man and this woman in holy matrimony...

CHARLES *looks back at* MATTHEW *who does a subtle nod – they've got something.*

> **VICAR:** *(Cont.)* Which is an honourable estate, instituted in the time of man's innocency...

> **CHARLES:** *(to* ANGUS*)* Back in a sec...

ANGUS *looks alarmed.*

> **VICAR:** Therefore if any man can show any just cause or impediment why they may not be lawfully joined together, let him speak now or forever hold his peace...

CHARLES *edges subtly down a side aisle.*

> **VICAR:** Do you promise to love her, comfort her, honour and keep her in sickness and in health, and forsaking all others, keep thee only unto her, for as long as ye both shall live?

MATTHEW *tiptoes across the back of the church.*

> **ANGUS:** I do.

MATTHEW *and* CHARLES *meet at the back for the subtle handover, without us seeing the rings.* CHARLES *however looks down – then up at* MATTHEW *–* MATTHEW *shrugs – 'best he could do'.*

> **LAURA:** ...To love and to cherish...

VICAR: Till death do us part.

LAURA: Till death do us part.

VICAR: And thereto I pledge thee my troth.

LAURA: And thereto I pledge thee my troth.

At that moment CHARLES *skids in next to* ANGUS.

VICAR: Do you have the ring?

The VICAR *moves towards him, holding open the bible,* CHARLES *takes a little step forward and puts the still unseen rings on the book. The* VICAR *looks slightly surprised.*

VICAR: With this ring I thee wed, with my body I thee worship and with all my worldly goods I thee endow...

ANGUS: With this ring I thee wed, with my body I thee worship and with all my worldly goods I thee endow...

ANGUS *slips the ring on to* LAURA's *finger. It is a big multi-coloured shiny heart.* ANGUS *looks startled.* CHARLES *plays innocent, and happy. Then* LAURA *slips hers onto* ANGUS's *hand – it is a skull and cross-bones.*

CUT TO: *A 38-year-old man with receding hair, reading pompously.*

GEORGE: 'If I speak with the tongues of men and of angels, but have not love, I am become a sounding brass, or a clanging cymbal.'

GARETH: Good point.

CUT TO: *A couple with an acoustic guitar, playing Barry Manilow's classic hit 'Can't Smile Without You'. It is the bride's sister and her boyfriend,* CLAUDIA *and* CRAIG, *filling in while the couple sign the register.*

CLAUDIA AND CRAIG:
'You know I can't smile without you
Can't smile without you.
I can't laugh, and I can't sing... '

GARETH *has his head in his hands in despair. It is one of the worst experiences of his life.* TOM *and* SCARLETT *sway merrily.*

CUT TO: *The newly-weds leaving the church, the toccata plays.*

19. EXT. WEDDING 1. COUNTRY CHURCH. DAY.

CHARLES *standing just outside as the guests leave. Everyone knows him.* CARRIE *passes...*

> **CHARLES: Great hat.**
>
> **CARRIE: Thanks – I bought it specially...**

She moves on, with a slightly wry smile. She's American. He likes her.

20. EXT. WEDDING 1. COUNTRY CHURCH. DAY.

The wedding photos are being taken. Three quick shots of the family. In the course of the shots, a 6-year-old boy goes under the skirt of the bride and emerges smiling. Then is hit.

Meanwhile, CHARLES's *friends gather on the sidelines, a real group, comfortable:* MATTHEW, GARETH, FIONA, SCARLETT, TOM, DAVID. *Also* BERNARD – TOM's *best friend.*

TOM: Splendid, I thought – what did you think?

BERNARD: I thought splendid – what did you think?

TOM: Splendid, I thought.

*

GARETH: Scarlotta – fabulous dress – the ecclesiastical purple and the pagan orange symbolising the magical symbiosis in marriage between the heathen and Christian traditions.

SCARLETT: *(Confused)* That's right.

*

CHARLES: Any idea who the girl in the black hat is?

They look across at CARRIE, *who is listening considerately to a grand-mother.*

FIONA: Name's Carrie.

CHARLES: Pretty.

FIONA: American.

CHARLES: Interesting.

FIONA: Slut.

CHARLES: Really?

FIONA: Used to work at Vogue. Lives in America now – only goes out with very glamorous people – quite out of your league.

CHARLES: Well, that's a relief. Thanks.

Cut to the bridal party now waving goodbye as they get into the big car.

GARETH: Right – reception!

21. EXT. COUNTRY HOUSE. DAY.

The guests are walking through a farmyard to a country house. There is a lovely, rural feeling to everything, as though the wedding is a harvest festival. There are pink bows on the sheep they pass. They chat as they walk.

TOM: Anyone else tread in a cowpat? No – thought not. See you in a mo.

FIONA: Do you think I'd hate him as much if he wasn't my brother?

TOM: Don't want to blow my chances for romance by smelling of dung all the way through the reception.

TOM rubs his foot violently against a bale of hay. Then another bale gently topples on to him. The others walk on down the long lawn.

FIONA: God. I never know what to say in these wretched line-ups.

GARETH: It's a cinch – just give a big warm hug and say the bride looks pregnant.

MATTHEW: Or you can stick with tradition and go for 'you must be very proud'.

FIONA: Heaven preserve us.

22. EXT. COUNTRY HOUSE. RECEPTION LINE. DAY.

Wife LAURA *is hugely gushy, laughy, hugging everyone. Husband* ANGUS *is smiling, which is unusual for him. Then there are the four parents. At the end stand various sisters, brothers and bridesmaids and* CHARLES.

> FIONA: *(So sincerely to the father of the bride)* **You must be very proud.**

> TOM: *(Slightly hay-covered)* **Hello.**

23. EXT. MARQUEE. RECEPTION. DAY.

A beautiful marquee, decked out with flowers and ribbons – full of tables, with a long table at the end on a slightly raised dais. Expensive, but with a nice homey feeling to it. The family are upper middle class: there are lots of guests wearing dark suits, not wedding coats – and there are lots of flower pattern dresses. Local people are also there – from the faithful farmhand to the lord lieutenant.

Throughout the reception, the background action should be full of the business of weddings: waiters and waitresses at work, band tuning up, people chatting and laughing.

CUT TO: CHARLES *winding through people. He spies* CARRIE, *but she is headed off by a good-looking man – she is clearly much fêted.*

CHARLES: **Bastard.**

He heads for the drinks table to stock up. By the time he turns, she's alone again. He makes it to her.

CHARLES: **O – hello. Want one of these?**

CARRIE: **Thank you.**

CHARLES: **Ahm...**

Just as he's searching for what to say, an acquaintance slips into shot: he's rather a stiff, 38-going-on-60 stockbroker.

JOHN: Hello, Charles.

CHARLES: Hello, dear John – how are you?...This is...

CARRIE: Carrie.

JOHN: Delighted, I'm John.

Tiny pause – who's to talk?

CHARLES: So, John – how's that gorgeous girlfriend of yours?

JOHN: She is no longer my girlfriend.

CHARLES: O dear – still, I wouldn't get too gloomy – rumour has it she never stopped bonking old Toby de Lisle, just in case you didn't work out.

JOHN: She is now my wife.

CHARLES: Excellent. Excellent. Congratulations.

CARRIE takes in totally that this is the most embarrassing moment and leaves them to it, amused.

CARRIE: Excuse me.

She walks away. Tiny pause.

> CHARLES: Ahm...any kids or anything, John? Do we hear the patter of tiny feet? No – plenty of time for that, isn't there. No hurry.

CUT TO: In a corner, CHARLES stands alone, then deliberately hits his head against the pole of the marquee, once. When he stands straight again, an old lady passes his line of vision. He clearly knows her, and smiles politely.

> CHARLES: Hi, how are you?

When she leaves his head sinks again. We notice that CARRIE is watching him.

CUT TO: FIONA, nearby, talking to an innocent-looking fellow with an odd-looking haircut.

> FIONA: My name's Fiona.
>
> GERALD: I'm Gerald.
>
> FIONA: What do you do?
>
> GERALD: I'm training to be a priest.
>
> FIONA: Good Lord. Do you do weddings?
>
> GERALD: Not yet – I will though, of course – jolly nerve-racking.
>
> FIONA: Rather like the first time one has sex.
>
> GERALD: Ahm, well, I suppose so...
>
> FIONA: Though rather less messy, of course...and far less call for condoms.
>
> GERALD: *(Embarrassed)* Aaahm...

CUT TO: CHARLES, *still alone.* DAVID *approaches.* DAVID *is deaf and talks to his brother* CHARLES *in sign language. They have always done it and* CHARLES *is very deft and comfortable with it.*

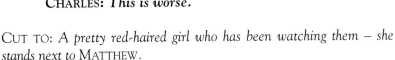

> DAVID: *How you doing?*
>
> CHARLES: *Remember that time you started Dad's boat and the propeller cut my leg to shreds?*
>
> DAVID: *Yes.*
>
> CHARLES: *This is worse.*

CUT TO: *A pretty red-haired girl who has been watching them – she stands next to* MATTHEW.

> SERENA: Who's that boy over there – in the grey?
>
> MATTHEW: His name's David.
>
> SERENA: He's something of a dish, isn't he?
>
> MATTHEW: I've always thought so.
>
> SERENA: Why were they... *(Mimes signing)*
>
> MATTHEW: The dish can't hear.
>
> SERENA: O. Gosh.
>
> MATTHEW: Silent, but deadly attractive.

A gong sounds…

> FATHER OF THE BRIDE: Ladies and gentlemen – dinner is served.

24. INT. MARQUEE. RECEPTION. DAY.

The friends: they sit down at their different tables. All have quite pleasant companions.

> TOM: Tom – splendid to meet you – very exciting.

Behind him, CARRIE is sat down by GEORGE, the pompous lesson reader.

*

John sits down uneasily beside his adulterous wife.

*

SCARLETT: **Hi – my name's Scarlett.** (*She gives the total stranger a kiss on the mouth.*) **Don't let me drink too much cos I get really flirty.**

She takes her first big gulp of wine.

*

CHARLES glides into his position on the long, raised-up top table and introduces himself to the OLD MAN next to him.

CHARLES: **How do you do – my name is Charles.**

OLD MADMAN: **Don't be ridiculous, Charles died twenty years ago.**

CHARLES: **Must be a different Charles, I think.**

OLD MADMAN: **Are you telling me I don't know my own brother?**

CHARLES: **No, no.**

CUT TO: *Wide shot of the eating arrangements. Along from CHARLES are the bride and groom, parents-in-law, uncles, and vicars. Knives and forks going into mouths.*

Sound of a spoon on glass: CHARLES *stands. He speaks in a very self-effacing manner…*

> CHARLES: Ladies and gentlemen – I'm sorry to drag you from your delicious desserts: there are just one or two little things I feel I should say as best man.

The guests turn to listen to him.

> CHARLES: (*Cont.*) This is only the second time I've ever been a best man. I hope I did the job all right that time – the couple in question are at least still talking to me. Unfortunately, they're not actually talking to each other – the divorce came through a couple of months ago.
>
> But I'm assured it had absolutely nothing to do with me. Apparently Paula knew that Piers had slept with her younger sister before I mentioned it in the speech.

CUT TO: CARRIE *laughing brightly – then back to* CHARLES.

> CHARLES: The fact that he'd also slept with her mother came as a surprise – but I think it was incidental to the nightmare of recrimination and violence that became their two-day marriage. Anyway – enough of that – my job today is to talk about Angus and there are no skeletons in his cupboard. Or so I thought…

Laughter.

> CHARLES: I'll come on to that in a minute – I would just like to say this – I am, as ever, in bewildered awe of anyone who makes the kind of commitment that Angus and Laura have made today. I know I couldn't do it – I think it's wonderful they can.
>
> So anyway, back to Angus and those sheep.

CUT ON TO.

> **CHARLES:** Ladies and gentlemen – if you'd raise your glasses – the adorable couple.

All stand and toast.

> **ALL: The adorable couple!**

> *Cheers as the couple kiss.*

> CUT TO: *The slightly dodgy rock 'n' roll band starting to play 'Crocodile Rock'.*

> *The newly-weds, LAURA and ANGUS, come out and dance. Everyone applauds. She dances rather exotically, he as though this is the first time he's ever heard pop music.*

> SCARLETT *starts dancing wildly but enthusiastically with* TOM, *the worst dancer in the world, but the keenest.*

> *Beside them is* GARETH *twisting with great vigour.*

> CHARLES *is clearly looking for* CARRIE – *but then there she is on the dance-floor with one of her dinner companions.* MATTHEW *comes up beside him.*

> **MATTHEW: I remember the first time I saw Gareth on the dance-floor, I feared lives would be lost.**

> GARETH *is doing a dance made popular by Saturday Night Fever.*

MATTHEW: Pretty girl, the one you can't take your eyes off. Is it love at first sight?

CHARLES *is slightly thrown by* MATTHEW's *perception.*

CHARLES: Good Lord no – it's the bloke she's dancing with – I used to play rugby with him at school – I'm just trying to remember which position he played in. Though let's say, for the sake of argument, one did take a fancy to someone at a wedding: do you think there really are people who can just go up and say, 'Hi, babe – name's Charles – this is your lucky night'.

MATTHEW: If there are, they're not English.

CHARLES: Quite – three weeks is about my question-popping minimum.

25. EXT. MARQUEE. SUNSET.

Later that night, around 9 pm. LAURA, *emotionally talking to and hugging some distant cousins.*

LAURA: You know I love you, Jean, don't you. I love you, I love you, and Mike, I've never met you before, but I love you very much, I really do.

ANGUS *remarks to* MATTHEW, *who stands next to him.*

ANGUS: Ignore her – she's drunk. *(Pause)* At least I hope she is. *(Worried pause)* Otherwise I'm in real trouble.

26. INT. MARQUEE. RECEPTION. NIGHT.

In the corners of the room people are a little worse for wear.

BERNARD *is speaking to the fulsome bridesmaid,* LYDIA.

BERNARD: How's it going, Lyds?

LYDIA: Bloody awful.

BERNARD: O dear. What's the prob?

LYDIA: I was promised sex – everybody said it: 'You be a bridesmaid, you'll get sex. You'll be fighting them off'. But not so much as a tongue in sight.

BERNARD: Well, look – I mean, if you fancy... ahm, anything, I could always...

LYDIA: O don't be ridiculous, Bernard – I'm not that desperate.

BERNARD: No, right, of course, fair enough: it's a good point.

27. EXT. COUNTRY HOUSE. NIGHT.

People are gathered to wave the married couple goodbye. As they head out, the bride throws her bouquet. SCARLETT *reaches for it,* FIONA *dodges it. It is caught by* LYDIA.

The couple approach the wedding car with a string of cans attached to it – and 'Just Married' and '3 Months Pregnant' in fake snow on the windscreen. They open the door, and a big white sheep with a bow on jumps out – a roar of delight.

A big cheer as they drive away.

CHARLES *heads disconsolately back into the marquee. The band plays 'Love is All Around'.*

28. INT. MARQUEE. NIGHT.

A very late-night atmosphere. SCARLETT, BERNARD, DAVID, SERENA. TOM *joins* CHARLES *keenly.*

TOM: Where are you staying tonight, Charles?

CHARLES: Scarlett and I are at some pub – the Lucky Boat, something like that. Aren't we all?

TOM: Ah – no – slight change of plan – the others are in fact coming back to my place: Nansy's in residence – might knock us up a quick plate of eggs and bac' over a late-night Scrabble. I wondered if you'd like to join.

CHARLES: Yes – that would be great – thanks very much – is there room for Scarlett ?

TOM: O absolutely. 137 rooms actually.

CHARLES: Tom – are you the richest man in England?

TOM: O – no, no. I believe we're about seventh. The Queen, obviously, and that Branson bloke is doing terribly well. Well, excellent news – I'll go tell Scarlett.

As TOM *walks away....*

TOM: That's unless you get lucky first.

CHARLES *smiles weakly – and suddenly,* CARRIE *is right beside him.*

CARRIE: Hi.

CHARLES *is taken aback.*

CHARLES: Hi. I thought you'd gone.

CARRIE: No – not yet. I was just wondering where you're staying tonight?

CHARLES: Well, I was staying at some pub, called the Lucky Boat, or something...

CARRIE: Boatman.

CHARLES: Right. But now I'm going to stay at some friend's house...with some friends. Well, I say 'house' – I think 'enormous castle' is a more accurate description.

CARRIE: O, that's too bad. I'm at the Boatman.

CHARLES: O.

Pause. She doesn't give CHARLES *quite enough time to recover. It's quite a direct invitation.*

CARRIE: Well, it was nice not quite meeting you. Great speech.

CHARLES: Thanks.

Long pause.

CARRIE: Well, I'm going now.

CHARLES: No, don't – we could meet now – the evening's just getting going.

They survey the fallen-bottle, toppled-chair mess.

CARRIE: I think we both know that's a big lie.

She walks away.

CHARLES: Fuck.

Later: the camera pans over the proceedings – CLAUDIA *and* CRAIG *are back with their unusual version of 'Stand By Your Man'. Two exhausted hugging couples are still on the dance floor, trying to dance to it. Couples are kissing. Drunk people are asleep.*

GARETH: I think the castle beckons. Tom, are you sober?

TOM: Absolutely. Orange juice all night.

TOM *then trips spectacularly. They walk out, jackets slung over their shoulders:* CHARLES, TOM, GARETH, MATTHEW, DAVID, FIONA, *picking up an exhausted* SCARLETT *as they go. They pass a couple kissing passionately. Hold on them. They split: it's* LYDIA *the bridesmaid and* BERNARD, *whom she so recently spurned. She's quite breathless.*

LYDIA: Bernard!

29. EXT. COUNTRY LANE. NIGHT.

It's a starry night. Wide beautiful shot of the countryside, TOM's *Land Rover winding down a country lane. From it ring the strains of 'Stand By Your Man'. They are having a lot of trouble with the high notes.*

CHARLES: Tom, can you stop the car?

The car stops dead.

CHARLES: Sorry, I think I might stay in that pub after all.

TOM: Why on earth?

CHARLES: Ahm...

All of them make a teasing police siren sound.

CHARLES: No, seriously, I'm doing some research into pubs with the word 'Boat' in the title. I hope to produce the definitive work.

TOM: O well, suit yourself.

CHARLES *is left standing in the middle of the road, in the middle of the night, in the middle of nowhere.*

As the car drives away – they start to shout the chorus of 'Can't Smile'.

CHARLES *is left totally alone.*

> CHARLES: **Right. Odd decision.**

And he heads back along the road.

30. EXT. TOWN . NIGHT.

A charming town high street. The Boatman is a pleasant, large pub hotel, white, with an archway through which cars can drive and park at the back.

31. INT. RECEPTION. THE BOATMAN. NIGHT.

It is by now about one in the morning. Very quiet. CHARLES *sees the bell to ring on the front desk, but just before ringing, looks left, and sees something.*

> CHARLES: **Hello?**

CARRIE *leans over – and looks at him quizzically.*

> CARRIE: **Hi.**
>
> CHARLES: **In the end it turned out there wasn't room for all of us, so...**
>
> CARRIE: **You said it was a castle.**
>
> CHARLES: **Yes, it is a castle. It's a very very small one. Tiny, in fact. Just one up, one down. Which is rare.**

Enter a late night WAITER.

WAITER: A drink, sir?

CHARLES: Yes, I'd like a glass of whisky, thanks. Do you want...?

CARRIE: Yes, sounds good.

CHARLES *turns to the* WAITER.

CHARLES: And another one for the lady.

WAITER *leaves and* CHARLES *turns back to address* CARRIE – *but she's disappeared. It's clear why when* GEORGE *enters, the confident, balding, plump, annoying man who read the lesson in church.*

GEORGE: You here too?

CHARLES: Hello...

GEORGE: You haven't seen Carrie have you?

CHARLES: *(In a fluster)* Who?

GEORGE: Carrie. American girl. Lovely legs. Wedding guest. Nice smell.

CHARLES: No – sorry.

GEORGE: Damn. Blast. I think I was in there.

CARRIE *pops up from behind the sofa and pulls a face – he very clearly was not 'in there'.*

GEORGE: Look, if you do see her, could you tell her I've gone up to my room?

CHARLES: Yes, yes...

WAITER *comes in, just as* GEORGE *is about to leave.*

WAITER: Your whisky, sir, and one for the...

CHARLES: Road, lovely.

GEORGE: Actually, I think I might have one of those. Mind if I join you?

CHARLES: No...that would be lovely.

GEORGE: (*To* WAITER) **Another whisky. And a cigar. Actually make that a bottle of whisky.** (*To* CHARLES) **Might as well settle in. Let's see if we can push on through till dawn, shall we?**

They settle, CHARLES *on the sofa,* GEORGE *in the chair.* CARRIE *looks out from behind another chair and looks humourously exasperated at* CHARLES.

GEORGE: Lovely wedding.

CHARLES: Yes.

GEORGE: I was at school with his brother Bufty – tremendous bloke. He was head of my house. Buggered me senseless. Still, taught me a thing or two about life.

Reaction off CHARLES.

GEORGE: Where do you know them from?

CHARLES: University.

GEORGE: O splendid, splendid. Yes. I didn't go myself...couldn't see the point. When you're working the money markets, what use are the novels of Wordsworth going to be, eh?

WAITER *re-enters formally.*

WAITER: Excuse me, sir – your wife says, could you come upstairs at once. Room Twelve in case you're so drunk you can't remember.

CHARLES: My wife?

WAITER: Yes, sir.

CHARLES: O – my wife!!!

GEORGE: You are drunk if you can't even remember you've got a wife!!

CHARLES: Yes... (*Does a little drunk mime – then, excusing himself*) **Do you mind, if I...?** (*Points upstairs*)

GEORGE: O no – off you go – best of luck. Lucky bachelor me, I think I'll have another search for that Katie creature.

CHARLES: Carrie.

GEORGE: That's the one. Damn fine filly. I think I'm in there.

32. INT. CORRIDOR. THE BOATMAN. NIGHT.

CHARLES *knocks on the door of Room 12.* CARRIE *opens it.* CHARLES *is slightly nervous.*

CARRIE: Hi.

CHARLES: Hello. Sorry about that.

CARRIE: No, that's fine – he was hard to get rid of.

CHARLES: Yes – so...maybe we could just skulk around here for a bit and then go back down.

CARRIE: That's a thought – I don't usually skulk a lot, but I suppose I could skulk if skulking were required. Do you skulk regularly?

CHARLES: No, I don't normally think of myself as a skulker, but...

CARRIE: Well, why don't you come in, and skulk for a while, and we'll see...

33. INT. ROOM 12. THE BOATMAN. NIGHT.

They are both inside the room. Pause.

CARRIE: I noticed the bride and groom didn't kiss in the church, which is kind of strange – where I come from, kissing is very big.

CHARLES: Is it? Yes, I think you're right – I think we are probably more reserved. 'You may now kiss the bride' isn't actually in the Book of Common Prayer.

CARRIE: I always worry I'd go too far...in the heat of the moment.

This is an acquiescent seduction – breaking through CHARLES's 3-week-question-popping qualities.

CHARLES: How far do you think too far would be then?

CARRIE: I don't know...maybe... (*Gives him a peck on the cheek*) that would be all right.

CHARLES: Yes – I think that would be fine.

CARRIE: In fact, it might be a bit dismissive. Maybe this... (*A kiss on the mouth*) would be better.

CHARLES: Yes. I think it would be dangerous to take it any further. I mean...

They are centimetres apart. It turns into a long kiss...

CHARLES: That might be taking it a little far.

The camera cuts across the room, and pans back to them.

CARRIE (V/O): What about this – do you think the vicar would think things had slipped just a little bit out of his control?

It's moments later – they are making love on the bed.

CHARLES: I think he might. This kind of thing is really more suited to the honeymoon than to the service itself.

CARRIE: Why do you think it's called 'honeymoon'?

CHARLES: I don't know – I suppose it's 'honey' because it's as sweet as honey – and 'moon' because it was the first time a husband got to see his wife's bottom.

She laughs – for all his early unsureness, she makes him relaxed, by being so totally relaxed herself. They kiss.

34. EXT. COUNTRYSIDE. DAWN.

The beautiful landscape outside waking up in the dawn. Birds rise from a bare field by a little village.

35. INT. ROOM 12. THE BOATMAN. DAY.

CARRIE is zipping up her bag. She stops and looks carefully at CHARLES, who is still asleep. He slowly wakes, opens his eyes, and looks up. Her face is caught in beautiful light.

CHARLES: What's happening?

CARRIE: I have to go.

CHARLES: Where?

CARRIE: America.

CHARLES: That is a tragedy.

CARRIE: Just before I go – when were you thinking of announcing the engagement?

CARRIE: Sorry – whose engagement?

CARRIE: Ours. I assumed since we'd slept together and everything, we'd be getting married. What did you think?

CHARLES: Well, I, gosh, yes, takes a lot of thinking about that kind of thing, obviously I ahm...

Then he suddenly sees she's smiling.

CHARLES: You're joking.

She nods and laughs.

> CHARLES: God, for a moment there I thought I was in 'Fatal Attraction'. I thought you were Glenn Close and I was going to get home and find my pet rabbit on the stove.

> CARRIE: No. But I think we both missed a great opportunity here. Bye.

And she's gone. He turns over, sinks his head into his pillow, and the alarm clock goes off again.

Wedding 2
AUGUST 1ST

36. INT. CHARLES'S BEDROOM. CHARLES & SCARLETT'S HOUSE. DAY.

CHARLES's hand reaches up and switches off the ringing alarm.

Caption: 3 months later.

You are cordially invited to attend the wedding of

Bernard & Lydia

St. Mary of The Fields, Cripplegate, London EC2

37. INT. SCARLETT'S BEDROOM. CHARLES & SCARLETT'S HOUSE. DAY.

SCARLETT's *room – she is asleep. We hear a loud shout outside.*

    CHARLES (V/O): **O fuck.**

CHARLES *rushes in in his boxer shorts. He shakes her and rushes out. Her eyes open. She sees her alarm clock.*

    SCARLETT: Fuck.

38. EXT. CHARLES & SCARLETT'S HOUSE. DAY.

The two of them sprint out the door – still dressing. SCARLETT *in a huge and ridiculous peach-coloured satin number.*

    CHARLES: Fuck.

    SCARLETT: Fuck.

They don't stop running.

    SCARLETT: Car or taxi?

    CHARLES: Taxi. We could never park.

39. EXT. BUSY STREET CORNER. DAY.

The two of them rush to look for a taxi. Ten seconds looking, to no avail.

    CHARLES: Car seems a good idea.

40. EXT. ANOTHER STREET. DAY.

Them at her car. It is clamped.

BOTH: Fuck.

41. EXT. BUSY STREET. DAY.

Two joggers are pacing each other, going fast – then, in full wedding gear, CHARLES and SCARLETT whip past them, her dress ballooning in the wind. In fact, a huge piece falls away. CHARLES makes to pick it up.

SCARLETT: Leave it – no-one'll notice.

42. EXT. WEDDING 2. CATHOLIC CHURCH. DAY.

They arrive still sprinting at a beautiful grand Catholic London church. Bells ring loudly.

CHARLES runs in. SCARLETT takes her place with a grin and dark glasses beside the wedding car.

43. INT. WEDDING 2. CATHOLIC CHURCH. DAY.

Exquisite, big, elegant church. There in a cluster are FIONA, MATTHEW, GARETH, DAVID. They've left a space for CHARLES.

CHARLES: Sorry I'm late. Traffic.

They all give him a look of total cynicism.

CHARLES: Yes...ahm...who is it today?

He studies the order of service in mock interest.

CUT TO: *The front. A young priest enters to conduct the service. It is* FATHER GERALD *from the last reception. He looks a little tense. His cape is slightly awkwardly slung over his shoulders. He seems to be rehearsing the service to himself. There are a nerve-racking number of prelates in big hats in attendance.*

CUT TO: TOM, *up in position as best man – he turns and gives* CHARLES *a little wave. Produces two rings from his pocket – pretends they're glasses – gives* CHARLES *a thumbs up.* CHARLES *smiles back.*

CUT TO: *Outside. Last minute fluttery adjustments to the bride's frock – a photo, then the organ begins and the bride and her father set off down the aisle to Handel's 'Arrival of the Queen of Sheba'. She is* LYDIA, *who kissed* BERNARD *at the end of the last wedding.*

Behind are two tiny satin peach bridesmaids, two pages, and two 25-year-olds in the same material. One of them is SCARLETT.

It is noticeable as she passes that her dress has no back, revealing her small blue pants. As she walks she also puts on a very unexpected curly orange wig, and, just at the last moment, removes her shades.

The bride arrives at the front – the father steps aside – BERNARD, *the groom, steps forward. He is smiling and nervous. After a last minute fluster removing his hat,* FATHER GERALD *begins.*

> FATHER GERALD: **In the name of the Father and of the Son and of the Holy Spirit. Amen.**
>
> ALL: **Amen.**
>
> FATHER GERALD: **Let us pray. Father – you have made the bond of marriage a holy mystery, a symbol of Christ's love for his church. Hear our prayers for Bernard and Lydia, through your son Jesus Christ, our Lord, who lives and reigns with you and the Holy Goat – Ghost – one God for ever and ever. Amen.**

MATTHEW leans over and whispers to CHARLES.

MATTHEW: It's his first time. Friend of the family.

CHARLES: Ah. Excellent.

They're all enjoying it.

FATHER GERALD: Bernard and Lydia – I shall now ask if you freely undertake the obligations of marriage. Bernard, repeat after me...I do solemnly declare...

BERNARD: I do solemnly declare...

FATHER GERALD: That I know not of any lawful impediment...

BERNARD: That I know not of any lawful impediment...

FATHER GERALD: Why I, Lydia...

BERNARD: Why I, Bernard...

CUT AWAY TO: CHARLES *and friends – loving it.*

CUT BACK TO:

FATHER GERALD: Sorry – why I Bernard Godfrey Saint John Delaney...

BERNARD: Why I Bernard *Geoffrey StJohn* Delaney... (*That's pronounced 'Sinjeon'*)

FATHER GERALD: May not be joined in matrimony to Lydia John Hibbott.

BERNARD: May not be joined in matrimony to Lydia *Jane* Hibbott.

FATHER GERALD *getting nervouser.*

FATHER GERALD: Lydia, repeat after me... I do solemnly declare...

LYDIA: I do solemnly declare...

FATHER GERALD: That I know not of any lawful impediment...

LYDIA: That I know not of any lawful impediment...

FATHER GERALD: Why I, Lydia *Jane* Hibbott...

LYDIA: Why I, Lydia *Jane* Hibbott...

FATHER GERALD: May not be johned in matrimony...

LYDIA: May not be *joined* in matrimony...

FATHER GERALD: To Bernard Geoffrey Sijjjern Delaney. (*It's the best he can do*)

LYDIA: To Bernard Geoffrey St John Delaney. (*Perfect Sinjeon once more*)

BERNARD *and* LYDIA *now join their right hands.*

FATHER GERALD: I call upon those persons here present to witness...

BERNARD: I call upon those persons here present to witness...

FATHER GERALD: That I, Bernard... (*Long pause*) Delaney...

BERNARD: (*Smiling*) That I, Bernard Delaney...

FATHER GERALD *smiles back with relief.*

FATHER GERALD: Do take thee, Lydia Jane Hibbott...

BERNARD: Do take thee, Lydia Jane Hibbott...

That went fine too – all smiles and relief.

FATHER GERALD: To be my awful wedded wife.

BERNARD: To be my *lawful* wedded wife.

FATHER GERALD: That's right. That's right. May Almighty God bless you all, the Father, the Son, and the Holy Spiggott – Spirit.

ALL: Amen.

GARETH: Bravo.

GARETH starts to applaud, thrilled they've made it through. The whole congregation joins in. GERALD is pretty delighted at how it went.

44. EXT. WEDDING 2. CATHOLIC CHURCH. DAY.

A series of snapshots of the happy couple. First 150 people, the hugest group of relatives ever. TOM is busy organising. Then 30. Then 15. Then a final snap just of the happy pair – except there is one collapsed grandmother just at the edge of frame.

45. INT. THE HOLBEIN HOTEL. RECEPTION ROOM. DAY.

The reception in an exclusive London hotel. A few faces we recognise. This is a very aristocratic wedding. All men are in full wedding gear: there's a lot of silk and lots of posh voices.

The bride is hooting and kissing.

CHARLES and GARETH and MATTHEW drinking and relaxed – experienced wedding guests.

GARETH: I've got a new theory about marriage. Two people are in love, they live together, and then, suddenly, one day, they run out of conversation. Totally. They can't think of a single thing to say to each other. That's it. Panic. Then suddenly it occurs to the chap that there is a way out of the deadlock...

CHARLES: Which is?

GARETH: He'll ask her to marry him.

CHARLES: Brilliant. Brilliant.

GARETH: Suddenly – they've got something to talk about for the rest of their lives.

CHARLES: So basically you're saying marriage is just a way of getting out of an embarrassing pause in conversation.

GARETH: Yup. The definitive ice-breaker.

TOM *passes by, looking busy about his duties.*

GARETH: Tom! How's the speech?

TOM: Pretty good, I think – something for everyone – tears, laughter...

GARETH: Excellent!

TOM *heads on*

CHARLES: I think it's a very good theory, Gareth.

MATTHEW: There is another argument, of course, that it does have something to do with true love.

CHARLES: Well, there's a thought.

46. EXT. THE HOLBEIN HOTEL. TERRACE. DAY.

CHARLES *reaches a drinks bar to order.*

CHARLES: Three glasses of brandy please...

Then suddenly, just at his shoulder...

CARRIE: Hi.

CHARLES *is stunned. There she is. Exquisite.*

CHARLES: Hello.

CARRIE: How are you?

CHARLES: Fine. Fine. Sorry – I'm...overwhelmed to see you. Don't go back to America. Please. I'll be back in two secs.

47. INT. THE HOLBEIN HOTEL. RECEPTION ROOM. DAY.

CHARLES *rushes back and gives the others their drinks.*

CHARLES: That's yours. That's yours. See you in five hours.

GARETH: Something happened?

CHARLES: Yes – it has a bit – this is a bloody great wedding you know.

48. EXT. THE HOLBEIN HOTEL. TERRACE. DAY.

CHARLES *bounds down the steps towards* CARRIE.

CHARLES: Hi. You look perfect. In fact, you probably *are* perfect. How are you?

CARRIE: I'm really well. Charles, I'd like you to meet Hamish, my fiance.

CHARLES: Excellent, excellent – how do you do, Hamish. Delighted to meet you. Charming surprise to find Carrie back in the country.

HAMISH *is an elegant, self-assured 50-year-old-man.*

HAMISH: Yes, well, she took a lot of persuading, I can tell you. Come on, darling, I told James I was going to get you – he'll begin to think I've totally lost control over you already.

CARRIE *takes his hand. Turns to* CHARLES *as she goes, very friendly.*

   CARRIE: **I'll see you later.**

CHARLES *is stunned with disappointment. He takes off his glasses and polishes them. He is suddenly very confused. This makes him very unhappy, for a reason he can't identify. It hits a deep chord of dissatisfaction – not just disappointment about her – something wider.*

49. INT. THE HOLBEIN HOTEL. RECEPTION ROOM. DAY.

CHARLES *sits alone.* MATTHEW *joins him.*

   MATTHEW: **How are you doing, Charles?**

CHARLES: Not great actually, suddenly. I don't know. I mean – what the hell's going on here – why am I always at weddings and never actually getting married, Matt?

MATTHEW: It's probably because you're a bit scruffy – or it could also be because you haven't met the right girl.

CHARLES: Ah, but you see – is that it? Maybe I have met the right girl – maybe I meet the right girls all the time. Maybe it's me.

MATTHEW: Nonsense.

CUT TO:

MASTER OF CEREMONIES: My lords, ladies and gentlemen. Dinner is served.

CUT BACK TO:

MATTHEW: Come on – odds on you meet your wife at dinner.

CHARLES: Yes.

50. INT. THE HOLBEIN HOTEL. BALLROOM. DAY.

CHARLES *in front of the seating plan.*

CHARLES: O my God.

CUT TO: CHARLES *sitting down – actually his table looks all right. It's 4 girls, 2 men, all presentable and his age. And* DAVID.

CHARLES: Hi.

ALISTAIR: Hello, I'm Alistair. I believe you know Veronica.

CHARLES: Yes. Hi, Vee. (*Nods to another girl*) Nicki. Great.

He's uneasy about something.

CUT TO: FIONA *sitting beside a rather grand middle-aged woman.*

MRS BEAUMONT: Tell me, are you married?

FIONA: No.

MRS BEAUMONT: Are you a lesbian?

FIONA: Good Lord – what made you say that?

MRS BEAUMONT: Well, it's one of the possibilities for un-married girls, and it is a bit more interesting than saying. 'O dear, just never found the right chap'. Eh?

FIONA: Quite right. Why be dull?

MRS BEAUMONT: Thank you.

FIONA: The truth is I have met the right person – only, he's not in love with me – and until I stop loving him, no one else stands a chance.

MRS BEAUMONT: Bad luck.

FIONA: Yes – isn't it? I was a lesbian once, at school – but only for about fifteen minutes, so I don't think it counts.

CUT TO: CARRIE – *enjoying herself with* MATTHEW *and* GARETH.

CUT TO: CHARLES'S *table. He looks over to* CARRIE *laughing with the others.*

> ALISTAIR: There are four hundred different kinds of tea, and that's not including all these so-called fruit teas. I took Veronica out to India at Christmas to have a look at the plantations.
>
> CHARLES: Excellent.

CHARLES *is just that little bit tense.*

> ALISTAIR: I believe you and her went out there once.
>
> CHARLES: That's right.
>
> VERONICA: Charles was vile – he insisted on cracking jokes all the time I was ill.
>
> CHARLES: I was just trying to cheer you up, Vee.
>
> NICKI: O, you're *that* Veronica.
>
> VERONICA: Which Veronica? Charlie... *(Panicking)*

CHARLES *tries to fend this all off.*

> CHARLES: Remember Bombay...?
>
> NICKI: When Charles and I were going out he told me he'd had this...'interesting' journey round India with 'Vomiting Veronica' – I think that was it.
>
> CHARLES: I don't remember ever mentioning it. Maybe...
>
> MARTHA: O come on, Charles, I don't think I've ever been out with anyone less discreet.

> *The true horror of the situation is now becoming clear.*

> CHARLES: I think that's probably a bit of an exaggeration, isn't it, Marth...

NICKI: It is not!

MARTHA: I remember you going on about this girl, Helena was it, whose mother made a pass at you.

VERONICA: I remember this! You couldn't work out whether it would be impolite not to accept her advances.

NICKI: That's right! Mrs Piggy – Helena was Miss Piggy, so her mother was Mrs Piggy.

CHARLES: I think perhaps...

They roar with laughter. CHARLES *is looking massively uncomfortable. Finally the girl beside him speaks.*

HELENA: We've both lost a lot of weight since then.

And pops a chocolate in her mouth. CHARLES *in total despair – a hammer sounds.*

CHARLES: Ah – great – speeches.

MASTER OF CEREMONIES: My lords, ladies and gentlemen – pray silence for the best man.

CUT TO: TOM, *standing, convinced he's on to a winner. Loud applause.*

TOM: Ahm...when Bernard told me he was getting engaged to Lydia, I congratulated him because all his other girl-friends had been such complete dogs – although, may I say how delighted we are to have so many of them here this evening...

GARETH *is loving it. He alone.*

TOM: I'm particularly delighted to see Camilla, who many of you will probably remember as the first person Bernard asked to marry him. If I remember rightly, she told him to 'sod off', and lucky for Lydia that she did!

51. INT. THE HOLBEIN HOTEL. RECEPTION ROOM. DAY.

Later. All of the friends gathered and relaxed on a big couch.

GARETH: We had the most adorable girl at our table – called Carrie…apparently her fiancée is awfully grand and owns half of Scotland. How are you?

CHARLES: I seem to be stuck in the wedding from hell. Ghosts of girlfriends past at every turn. The next thing you know, I'll bump into Henrietta and the horror will be complete.

From behind him comes a voice.

HENRIETTA: Hello Charles.

He turns around, and there is a strained-looking girl.

CHARLES: Hello, Hen. How are you?

Pause. Then her face just collapses into tears…

CHARLES: *(Sympathetically)* O Hen…

HELENA: Why can't you just leave her alone – haven't you hurt her enough?

CHARLES: Excuse me – I think I better be where other people are not.

As CHARLES *walks out, he passes* SERENA: *she approaches* DAVID. *She eases up to him, as before, via the canapés. She stands opposite him.*

SERENA: Hello. (*Then she starts to sign, very slowly.*) **I'm S-e-r-e-n-a.**

DAVID *smiles sweetly.*

DAVID: *Hello.*

SERENA: *I'm just learning. I'm probably naking tols of nistakes.*

DAVID *shakes his head.*

DAVID: *No, perfect. Perfect. Would you like to dance?*

SERENA: *Yes. That would be mice.*

52. INT. HOLBEIN HOTEL. CORRIDOR. NIGHT.

CHARLES, *upstairs with the sound of the party in the background – he looks along a corridor, then nips into a little room to be alone.*

53. INT. HOLBEIN HOTEL. ROOM. NIGHT.

It contains just a bed and a dressing table. On the cupboard hangs a suit. CHARLES *crosses to the window.*

54. INT. HOLBEIN HOTEL. ROOM WINDOW. NIGHT.

CHARLES *stands at the window which overlooks a London street. Below he sees* CARRIE *emerge into the light of a street lamp – she looks beautiful, as she stands on the pavement with* HAMISH, *while a doorman hails a cab.* CHARLES *yearns.*

55. INT. HOLBEIN HOTEL. BALLROOM. NIGHT.

SERENA *and* DAVID *dance, the quintessence of romance.*

54. (CONT.) INT. HOLBEIN HOTEL. ROOM. NIGHT.

There is a sound – CHARLES *turns around, and sees the door opening.* BERNARD *and* LYDIA *enter the room, noisily kissing – they don't see him. It is in fact the room for changing into their going-away clothes.*

Charles is a little worried by this. There is no doubt they are on the point of having sex on the bed. He begins to sneak out of the room, cautiously.

> LYDIA: **Wait a minute, this is no fun! I want to see my lovely husband.**

The light goes on. They are on the bed – LYDIA on top, BERNARD almost concealed under her wedding dress – and CHARLES is stranded directly behind them, frozen like a rabbit in the headlamps. Then slowly he eases himself towards a side door, and exits.

LYDIA: Who's a very bad bridegroom indeed?

56. INT. HOLBEIN HOTEL. BALLROOM. NIGHT.

People are dancing – the camera finds SCARLETT under a table with her 8-year-old fellow bridesmaid, FREDA. SCARLETT talks to her straight, as she does to everyone.

SCARLETT: Have you got a boyfriend?

FREDA: Yes.

SCARLETT: What's his name?

FREDA: Dolph. He's good at table tennis. What about you?

SCARLETT: No. 'Fraid not.

FREDA: Why not?

SCARLETT: I don't know – most of the blokes I fancy think I'm stupid and pointless, so they just bonk me and leave me. And the kind of blokes that do fancy me, I think are drips – I can't even be bothered to bonk them. Which does sort of leave me a bit nowhere.

FREDA: What's 'bonking'?

SCARLETT: Well, it's a bit like table-tennis – only with slightly smaller balls.

57. INT. HOLBEIN HOTEL. BEDROOM. NIGHT.

The couple are still making love. The door CHARLES *exited by swings open. It is in fact a sink concealed in a cupboard.* CHARLES *is crouching there. Not happy.*

There is an orgasm in the background. CHARLES *checks his watch. It's a long wait, not in ideal conditions.*

BERNARD: O, I love my wife.

LYDIA: I...love...my...husband!

BERNARD *sighs contentedly. In his cupboard,* CHARLES *looks relieved.*

BERNARD: Better be getting back.

CHARLES *nods.*

LYDIA: Or we could just wait a few minutes, and have another go.

CHARLES *shakes his head in intense worry.*

BERNARD: You naughty little rabbit.

CUT TO: BERNARD *and* LYDIA *on the bed.* CHARLES *politely steps out from the cupboard. He walks past them. They are very surprised. He holds up a pencil.*

CHARLES: **Found it.**

58. INT. HOLBEIN HOTEL. CORRIDOR. NIGHT.

As CHARLES *shuts the door behind him, he turns and bumps straight into* HENRIETTA.

HENRIETTA: **Charles, we must talk.**

CHARLES: *(Trapped, but kindly)* **Right, right.**

HENRIETTA: **The thing is, Charlie, I've spoken to lots of people about you.**

CHARLES: **O God.**

HENRIETTA: **...and everyone agrees – you're in real trouble, Charles...**

CHARLES: **Am I?**

HENRIETTA: **You see, you're turning into a sort of serial monogamist – one girlfriend after another – yet you'll never really love anyone, because you never let them near you.**

CHARLES: **On the contrary, Hen...**

HENRIETTA: **You're affectionate to them, and sweet to them ...you were even sweet to me although you thought I was an idiot.**

CHARLES: **I did not...**

HENRIETTA: **You did. I thought U2 was a type of submarine.**

CHARLES: **Well, in a way you were right – their music has a very naval quality...**

HENRIETTA: **Be serious Charles! You must give people a**

chance. You don't have to think, 'I must get married' – but you mustn't start every relationship thinking, 'I *mustn't* get married'.

CHARLES: Hen, you know me – most of the time I don't think at all – I just potter along.

HENRIETTA: O Charlie – (*she suddenly puts her arms around him*) – O God – the way you used to look at me. I just misread it, that's all – all the time I thought you were going to propose – but all the time you were just working out how to leave – O God…this is ridiculous.

She walks away. CHARLES *is left, slightly stunned. He turns…and there is* CARRIE.

CARRIE: Having a good night?

CHARLES: Yes, it's right up there with my father's funeral for sheer entertainment value. I thought you'd gone.

CARRIE: No – Hamish had to take the Edinburgh sleeper. I'm off now. Keep me company?

59. EXT. LONDON STREET. NIGHT.

A taxi drives through the streets of London.

60. INT. TAXI. NIGHT.

CARRIE *and* CHARLES *sit in the cab. Quiet.* CARRIE *taps on the window to stop the car.*

CARRIE: You want to come up for a night cap?

CHARLES: Are you sure?

CARRIE: (*Teasing him confidently*) Yes – I think we can risk it. I'm pretty sure I can resist you – you're not that cute.

CHARLES: (*Chastened*) OK. Yes. Great.

61. EXT. EARLY MORNING. LONDON. THE THAMES.

The city looks grey and beautiful.

62. INT. CARRIE'S BEDROOM. DAWN.

Dawn coming into CARRIE's bedroom. Love theme plays. CHARLES and CARRIE lie awake in bed together.

Cut to CHARLES putting on his wedding coat. He watches CARRIE as she lies, half awake, half asleep. At her most beautiful. Her eyes open. A long moment. Then quietly he leaves the room.

SEPTEMBER 1ST

63. INT. CHARLES'S BEDROOM. DAY.

His door opens. It is SCARLETT. She carries a tray.

> **SCARLETT: Morning, Charles – breakfast's up. Sorry it's a bit burnt.**

CHARLES wakes. They both settle down to breakfast on his bed, eating toast and sipping tea.

> **SCARLETT: What are you up to today?**

CHARLES: I'm taking advantage of the fact that for once in my entire life it's Saturday and I don't have a wedding to go to. All I have to do is not be late for David.

CHARLES *opens a big white letter.*

SCARLETT: I thought I might go for a job. There's this new shop called Spank that wants a sales assistant. I think I'd be great. They sell all this funny rubber stuff.

CHARLES: O no – another wedding invitation. And a list – lovely!

SCARLETT: They say rubber's mainly for perverts – I don't know why – I think it's very practical actually. I mean you spill anything on it and it just comes off. I suppose that could be why the perverts like it. Are you all right?

CHARLES *isn't concentrating. He's thrown by the contents of the invitation.*

CHARLES: Yes... It's that girl... Carrie – remember? The American...

64. INT. EXPENSIVE STORE. DAY.

CHARLES *walks into an expensive gift store. It is full of ceramic tigers, exotic carpets, woven baskets, beautiful silks, wooden carvings. He approaches an assistant. She is very snooty. She feels* CHARLES's *shorts and sneakers don't fit in with the spirit of the store.*

CHARLES: Excuse me, sorry to interrupt. Do you have the wedding list for Banks?

ASSISTANT: Certainly, sir – lots of beautiful things around the £1000 mark.

CHARLES: What about things round the £50 mark?

ASSISTANT: You could get that pigmy warrior over there...

CHARLES: This? Excellent.

ASSISTANT: If you can find someone else to chip in the other £3,950.

CHARLES *smiles*.

ASSISTANT: Or our carriers bags are £1.50 each – why don't you just get 33 of them?

CHARLES: Actually, I think I'll probably leave it. Thanks very much. You've been very...ahm...

He turns and bumps straight into CARRIE. *She's dressed very casually and looks very different: plainer, but still lovely. He's startled. She's in a very good mood.*

CARRIE: Watcha get?

CHARLES: (*Surprised remark*) Nothing yet – just...deciding.

CARRIE: It's nice to see you.

CHARLES: It's nice to see *you*.

CARRIE: This present thing is great. I should have gotten married years ago. (*To the* ASSISTANT) Anybody go for the pygmy?

ASSISTANT: The young man was thinking about it.

CHARLES *nods thoughtfully*.

CARRIE: O no – just get me an ashtray. Are you free for about a half hour?

CHARLES: Yes – I'm supposed to meet my brother, but...I can be a bit late.

CARRIE: Good. Come with me. You have an important decision to make.

65. INT. DRESS SHOP. DAY.

CHARLES *stands in a rather stylish, unusual-looking dress shop. 'But Not For Me' plays.*

CARRIE (V/O): Now the crucial thing is that you mustn't laugh.

CHARLES: OK. Right.

She swirls in in a typical...wedding dress. She is, despite herself, quite shy about it.

CARRIE: What do you think?

He looks at her, and then laughs gently... As if there's any question...

CHARLES: Divine.

CARRIE: Bit of a meringue?

CHARLES *acknowledges it is...*

CARRIE: Don't worry – we've only just begun.

*

CARRIE *in a wedding dress that is just trousers, an open coat and a bra. Sexy.*

CARRIE: What do you think?

CHARLES: You're kidding.

CARRIE: But it would be wonderful, wouldn't it? Maybe next time.

*

She walks out – it's a little Bo Peep number – lots of lace and silk bows.

CARRIE: What do you think?

CHARLES: Ahm...

CARRIE: I knew it.

She goes back in.

CHARLES: But if you could find a little staff it would be great for looking after sheep.

CARRIE *pops back out.*

CARRIE: Don't be rude.

*

She emerges in something slinky and outrageously slight.

CARRIE: It's a bit sexy this.

CHARLES: If I were your husband, I would die of pride... You may be right – it is dangerous – there's nothing in the world more off-putting at a wedding than a priest with an enormous erection.

66. INT. CAFE. DAY.

They sit in a cafe, a pot of tea between them. Outside, it is pouring with rain.

CHARLES: One strange thing is thinking you'll never sleep with anyone else. You don't think you'll be unfaithful?

CARRIE: No. Not once I'm married – I've told Hamish I'll kill him if he is – so I guess I better stick to that.

CHARLES: Quite right.

CARRIE: Anyway – I reckon I've had a fair run at it.

CHARLES: What is a fair run these days, down your way?

CARRIE: O, I don't know – more than...one.

CHARLES: Come on – tell me – I've seen the dress – we have no secrets now.

CARRIE: Well...

At first she's unwilling, but then she gets drawn in, counting them out on her fingers. Music threads in and out.

CARRIE: First one, of course – not easily forgotten. Kind of nice. Two – hairy back. Three. Four. Five. Six – was on my birthday. In my parents' room.

CHARLES: Which birthday?

CARRIE: Seventeen.

CHARLES: We've only reached seventeen?

CARRIE: I grew up in the country – lots of rolling around in haystacks. Ok – seven – mmmm. Eight – *(mimes half an inch)* – unfortunately – it was quite a shock. Nine – against a fence – very uncomfortable – don't try it...

CHARLES: I won't.

CARRIE: Ten – was gorgeous –
just heaven – he was wonderful...

CHARLES: I hate him.

CARRIE: Eleven – obviously, in the
circumstances, disappointing. Twelve
through seventeen – the university years
– sensitive, caring, intelligent boys: sexually speaking, a real low patch. Eighteen
– broke my heart. Years of yearning.

CHARLES: I'm sorry.

CARRIE: After which came nineteen – who I don't remember, but my room-mate said we definitely did it – twice.
Then twenty – God – I can't believe I've reached twenty.
Twenty-one – elephant tongue. Twenty-two – kept falling
asleep. That was my first year in England.

CHARLES: I do apologise.

CARRIE: Twenty-three and twenty-four together, that was
something...

CHARLES: Seriously?

CARRIE: Twenty-five – gorgeous – Frenchman. Twenty-six
– dreadful – Frenchman. Twenty-seven – now that was a
mistake.

CHARLES: Suddenly at twenty-seven you make a mistake?

CARRIE: He kept screaming – it was very off-putting – I
nearly gave up on the whole thing. But Spencer changed
my mind, that's twenty-eight – his father – twenty-nine...

CHARLES mouths 'Spencer's father!'

CARRIE: Then thirty – urgh. Thirty-one – O my god.
Thirty-two – was lovely. And then my fiancé, that's thirty-
three.

CHARLES: Wow! So I came...after your fiancé?

CARRIE: No, you were thirty-two.

CHARLES is a little flattered.

CARRIE: So there you go – less than Madonna, more than Princess Di – I hope. And how about you – how many have you slept with?

CHARLES: Christ, nothing like that many. Ahm. I don't know what the fuck I've been doing with my time actually. Work probably – that's it. Work. Work. I have been working late, a lot.

She laughs. Then both of them just stop talking. Something's happened. A serious pause.

CHARLES: I wish I'd rung you. But then you never rang me. You ruthlessly slept with me twice, and never rang me.

Pause.

CHARLES: O bollocks! (*Looks at his watch*) Help me, please – please.

67. EXT. NATIONAL FILM THEATRE. DAY.

DAVID is waiting outside the N.F.T. As CHARLES and CARRIE approach DAVID signs from afar.

DAVID: *You're no longer my brother – you're just some git I once met.*

CHARLES: Carrie, this is David, my brother. *This is Carrie.*

CARRIE: Hi.

CHARLES: *We were buying her a wedding dress.*

DAVID: *Pathetic excuse. Who's she marrying?*

CHARLES: *Some total penis.*

DAVID: *What is it about penises that they get such great wives?*

CARRIE *looks to* CHARLES *to translate it.*

CHARLES: I'm just telling him about you marrying Hamish – and he said it couldn't have happened to a nicer fellow – so that's nice.

DAVID: *Didn't you do it with her once?*

CHARLES: *(To* CARRIE*)* Where are you doing it?

CARRIE: Scotland.

CHARLES: Yes.

DAVID: *Beautiful breasts.*

CHARLES: He says that's a beautiful place. Hilly.

CARRIE: *(To* DAVID*)* You should come to the wedding too – I want as many friends as possible to make up for the gruesome stiffs that Hamish knows. Well, you better go in. Bye. Bye.

CHARLES: Bye.

They watch her as she walks away.

CHARLES: *Come on, we're late.*

They walk into the film theatre. Then, 5 seconds later…

CHARLES (V/O): Fuck it!

And he sprints out, up the stairs and after her…

68. EXT. THE EMBANKMENT. DAY.

CHARLES *runs after* CARRIE, *beside the river. It is sunny again. He finally catches and stops her.*

CHARLES: Ahm look –

She turns.

CHARLES: Sorry. Sorry. I just – this is a really stupid question – particularly in view of our recent shopping excursion – but I just wondered if by any chance – I mean, obviously not, because I am just some git who's only slept with *(confessing)* nine people, but I just wondered – I really feel...ahm... In short, to recap in a slightly clearer version – in the words of David Cassidy, in fact, while he was still with the Partridge Family – 'I think I love you', and I just wondered whether by any chance you wouldn't like to...no, no, of course not – I'm a idiot, he's not. Excellent. Excellent. Fantastic. Lovely to see you. Sorry to disturb – better get on.

He turns away.

CHARLES: Fuck.

CARRIE: That was very romantic...

CHARLES: Well, I thought it over a lot, you know, I wanted to get it just right... Important to have said it, I think.

CARRIE: Said what exactly?

CHARLES: Said...you know – what I just said – about... David Cassidy.

She moves forward.

CARRIE: You're lovely.

And kisses him.

Pause. They do not move. Then she walks away, looking back one time. He is left alone on the Embankment, Waterloo Bridge behind him.

Wedding 3

SEPTEMBER 28TH

You are cordially invited to attend the wedding of

Hamish & Carrie

The Chapel of Glenthrist Castle, Perthshire, Scotland

Caption: A month later.

69. EXT. SCOTLAND. DUSK.

A stormy mountain and loch, mist, rain, a rumble of thunder.

70. EXT. WEDDING 3. SCOTTISH CHURCH. DUSK.

A car drives along a path, then stops outside a small chapel, glowing warmly from inside. It is dusk, still except for the sound of a formal voice from inside. Charles leaps out – a replay of his traditional lateness. He takes off a thick jumper to put on a wedding coat.

71. INT. WEDDING 3. SCOTTISH CHURCH. DUSK.

Candles completely fill the church: it's like a fairy-tale. CARRIE stands at the altar, beautiful and serious behind her veil.

VICAR: Into this holy estate these two persons now desire to enter. Wherefore, if anyone can show any just cause why they may not lawfully be joined together in marriage, let him now declare it.

There is a bang at a side door. It is CHARLES.

CHARLES: *(Mouthing)* **Sorry.**

The service continues.

VICAR: Please rise. Do you, Hamish, take this woman Caroline to be your wedded wife – and do you, in the presence of God and before this congregation, promise and covenant to be to her a loving and faithful husband until God shall separate you by death?

HAMISH: I do.

CHARLES *makes his way to the back of the church.*

VICAR: Do you, Caroline, take this man Hamish to be your wedded husband – and do you, in the presence of God and before this congregation, promise and covenant to be to him a loving and faithful wife until God shall separate you by death?

CARRIE: I do.

CUT TO: CHARLES *taking it in.*

CHARLES: *(Last gasp of exhausted defeat)* **Fuck-a-doodle-doo.**

72. EXT. WEDDING 3. SCOTTISH CHURCH. EVENING.

Through an avenue of torches, guests walk to the reception. The church is in the grounds of the Scottish manor HAMISH *owns. Bagpipes play.*

The receiving line. Lots of men in kilts and women in very full dresses.
CHARLES *shakes hands down the line – best man,* HAMISH, *then* CARRIE.

> CHARLES: *(To Carrie)* **You looked beautiful. Not a meringue in sight.**
>
> CARRIE: **Thanks.**

He moves on into the main hall and…

> CHARLES: **Blimey.**

74. INT. SCOTTISH MANOR HOUSE. GRAND HALL. EVENING.

The hall is grand and Scottish – servants in highland finery, axes and spears on the wall, Scottish lasses reeling in the middle. GARETH *comes up behind him.*

> GARETH: **O bravo – it's Brigadoon. It's bloody Brigadoon!**

He dances on into the hall.

CUT TO: *The friends – together in a doorway.* GARETH *at his most exuberant. They have champagne.*

> GARETH: **Dear old things – as you know, I've always been proud that there's not a wedding ring between the lot of us. But with the passing of the years, it's suddenly beginning to distress me. I'd like to go to the wedding of someone I really loved for a change.**
>
> TOM: **Well, don't blame me: I've asked practically everyone I know.**

SCARLETT: You haven't asked me.

TOM: Haven't I?

SCARLETT: No.

TOM: Well, Scarlett...would you like to?

SCARLETT: No, thank you. It was very nice of you to ask.

TOM: Well, any time.

GARETH: Quite right, Tom, quite right. That's the spirit. Tonight, these are your orders – go forth and conjugate – find husbands and wives.

TOM: Excellent plan. What do you think, Fifi – spot a potential hubby in the throng?

FIONA: Bugger off, Tom.

TOM: Quite right.

GARETH: A toast before we go into battle. True love – in whatever shape or form it may come – may we all in our dotage be proud to say 'I was adored once too'.

ALL: True love!

CUT TO: *Guests dancing,* TOM *talking to a very pretty woman.*

TOM: Apparently an enormous number of people actually bump into their future spouses at weddings...which is interesting.

MARRIED WOMAN: Yes, I met my husband at a wedding.

TOM: (*Disappointed*) Ah. (*He takes a huge gulp of drink*) Good Lord, I seem to have finished my drink. If you'll excuse me...

CUT TO: SCARLETT – *standing beside the best-looking man at the wedding.*

SCARLETT: Hello, my name's Scarlett. Named after Scarlett O'Hara, but much less trouble. What's your name?

AMERICAN GOOD-LOOKER: My name's Rhett.

SCARLETT: No – not really?!

AMERICAN GOOD-LOOKER: No, not really. In fact it's Chester.

SCARLETT: You kidder – I always imagine Americans are going to be dull as shit – and of course you're not, are you? Steve Martin's American, isn't he?

CHESTER: Yes, he is.

SCARLETT: You're lovely.

CUT TO: *A little later –* CHARLES *on his own. A voice comes from behind him…*

HENRIETTA: Hello, Charles.

CHARLES: O Hen, hi, look, I'm sorry. I couldn't really bear a scene today. I know we've probably got tons to talk about and all that...

HENRIETTA: Did I behave that atrociously last time?

CHARLES: Well, you remember the shower scene in 'Psycho'?

HENRIETTA: Yes.

CHARLES: Scarier.

She laughs. She is in a good playful mood – you can now see why they might have once gone out – they are comfortable as old boyfriend and girlfriend.

CHARLES: O Hen, I'm depressed – how are you?

HENRIETTA: Well, cheerful actually – I weigh almost nothing and I've got a divine new boyfriend.

CHARLES: Perhaps you were right, Hen – perhaps we should have got married.

HENRIETTA: God, no. Marry you and I'd have to marry your friends – and I'm not sure I could take Fiona.

CHARLES: Fiona loves you.

HENRIETTA: Fiona calls me Duckface.

CHARLES: I never heard that.

HENRIETTA *knows he's lying.*

HENRIETTA: Come to lunch – give me a ring... (*Pecks him gently on the cheek*) Still cute.

She walks away. FIONA *slips in next to* CHARLES.

FIONA: How's Duckface?

CHARLES: Good form actually. Not too mad.

FREDERICK, THE BEST MAN: Ladies and gentlemen, the bride and groom.

They watch CARRIE *and* HAMISH *come on to the dance floor, accompanied by bagpipes and great applause. She begins to dance a formal, romantic Scottish dance with* HAMISH.

> FIONA: You like this girl, don't you?
>
> CHARLES: Yes, yes – it's a strange thing when at last it happens...and she's marrying someone else.

That was a sentence spoken without irony to a true friend.

> CHARLES: How about you, Fifi – you identified a future partner for life yet?
>
> FIONA: No need really. The deed is done. I've been in love with the same bloke for ages.
>
> CHARLES: Have you? Who's that?
>
> FIONA: *(Very casually)* You, Charlie.

A moment of stillness. They move into the next room. She takes a puff on her cigarette.

> FIONA: It's always been you, since first we met – o – so many years ago. I knew the first moment. Across a crowded room – or lawn in fact.

Pause.

> FIONA: Doesn't matter. Nothing either of us can do on this one. Such is life.

Pause.

> FIONA: 'Friends' isn't bad, you know. 'Friends' is quite something.

CHARLES *is shocked – he takes her hand.*

CHARLES: O Fi... Not all easy, is it.

FIONA: No. No. Just forget this business. Not to be.

At which moment, MATTHEW *enters.* FIONA *pretends nothing has happened.*

FIONA: Matthew darling. Where's Gareth?

MATTHEW: Torturing Americans.

FIONA: How thoughtful of him.

CUT TO: GARETH, *in conversation with an orange-haired American lady.*

CARRIE'S AUNT: Do you actually know Oscar Wilde?

GARETH: Not personally, no – but I do know someone who could get his fax number for you. Shall we dance?

CUT TO: *Ferociously exuberant dancing with* GARETH *and the now slightly startled American matron – he twirls her, he swings her, he hugs her.* TOM *is now dancing and gives the fruity eye to every girl he meets.*

CUT TO: GARETH *as he returns, hot from his dancing.* FIONA *and* CHARLES *are together.*

GARETH: Any rings on fingers?

FIONA: O, Gareth, you don't know how lucky you are – finding someone to marry is a very tricky business.

CHARLES *takes her meaning – they are in the same boat, together.*

GARETH: It's hell out there – Matthew's trapped with an evangelist from Minnesota.

CUT TO: MATTHEW *with a big man in a tartan blazer: he has his eyes closed and his hand on* MATTHEW'*s shoulder. He may be exorcising him.* MATTHEW *looks quizzical.*

> FREDERICK: **My lords, ladies and gentlemen – please charge your glasses. First, and rather unusually, we have…the bride.**

Enthusiastic applause.

> GARETH: **Excellent. I love this girl.**

CHARLES *looks up at* GARETH – *who looks back at him carefully – he now knows* CHARLES'*s secret.*

CUT TO: CARRIE *and* HAMISH *at the end, on a raised platform.*

> CARRIE: **Thank you. First of all I'd like to thank all of you who've flown in from the States. I'm really touched. And as for the rest of you – I would have thought the fact that lots of frightful Americans were flying in was the perfect excuse for staying away – so I thank you too.**

CHARLES *looks at her with love.*

> CARRIE: **If my darling Dad had been here today, he would have been speaking now – and I know what he would have said – 'Great dress, babe, but why the hell are you marrying the stiff in the skirt?'**

TOM *roars with laughter – he's very impressed at her cheek.*

> CARRIE: **And I would have given him the same answer that I give you – because I love him. As John Lennon said, who died the same year as my Dad, 'Love is the answer – and you know that for sure.'**

She kisses HAMISH. *They all clap.* CHARLES *can't believe he let her go.*

CARRIE: O, and one more thing – someone here told me confidentially that if things with Hamish didn't work out, that he would step in. I just wanted to say, 'thanks and I'll keep you posted'.

It's an outrageous thing to say and HAMISH *roars with laughter.* CHARLES *looks at her. In the background* GARETH *cries 'bravo'.*

FREDERICK: Now, my lords, ladies and gentlemen, Sir Hamish Banks.

HAMISH *is smooth, confident in his years and social position.*

HAMISH: Anyone involved in politics over the past twenty years has got used to being upstaged by a woman. But I didn't expect it to happen to me on my wedding day.

GARETH *seems to stumble.*

HAMISH: However I must also say that I'm quite happy to be upstaged by this woman for the rest of my life.

And now GARETH *falls violently, full to the floor, knocking a tray, making a slight clatter.*

HAMISH: O dear, is that some barracking at the back – again, something we politicians are used to.

CHARLES *moves to* GARETH, DAVID *and* TOM *are with him.*

CHARLES: Find a doctor.

TOM: OK.

Everyone else is still listening to HAMISH.

HAMISH: First of all, I want to extend my compliments to the bridesmaids – you did your duties superbly – and obviously I intend to use you every time I get married from now on.

CUT TO: GARETH. *The doctor – a wedding guest in black tie – is right there. He has a feel of* GARETH's *neck pulse.*

CUT TO: MATTHEW, *contentedly listening to the speech on the other side of the room.*

75. INT. SCOTTISH MANOR HOUSE. DRAWING ROOM. NIGHT.

They carry GARETH *into an empty room, and lay him on the floor.* HAMISH's *voice can still be heard in the background. There is a sharp contrast between the two rooms – one absolutely packed and full of laughter. The other still, with six small figures alone in a big space.*

CHARLES *cradles* GARETH's *head.* FIONA *arrives.* TOM *is standing with his hands behind his neck. There is a kerfuffle at the door, and* SCARLETT *sprints to them.*

And at that moment, GARETH *dies.*

76. INT. SCOTTISH MANOR HOUSE. GRAND HALL. NIGHT.

CHARLES, *his face white, walks through the crowds of people laughing.* HAMISH *still talking in the background…*

> HAMISH: I do remember the first time I set eyes on Caroline, I thought to myself – if, by any chance she's short-sighted, I might just be happy for the rest of my life. I thought I could see my future for the first time – and I knew it would be a joyful one, for years and years to come.

CHARLES *sees* MATTHEW *and walks towards him. Just before he reaches him, he hesitates – it's a hard moment.*

The guests begin to sing 'For He's a Jolly Good Fellow'.

CHARLES *moves forward, takes* MATTHEW's *arm, and whispers to him. Cut away as we take in* MATTHEW's *reaction to the news.*

A funeral

77. EXT. GARETH'S PARENTS' HOUSE. DAY.

A small house in an industrial landscape. MATTHEW leads out GARETH's father and mother to a waiting funeral car. They get in and it drives slowly away.

78. EXT. FUNERAL CHAPEL. DAY.

CHARLES, DAVID, SCARLETT and TOM enter the small stone chapel.

79. INT. FUNERAL CHAPEL. DAY.

They enter and move through the congregation. It is very different from the other congregations. Half the chapel is filled with modestly dressed relatives of GARETH's, from the estate behind the chapel. There are aunts, uncles, old teachers. Also a group of gay friends, and faces we recognise: ANGUS, LYDIA, BERNARD, LAURA.

CARRIE is there, near the back. She looks plain, un-made up – a beautiful, but rather startling contrast to the high flush of her wedding day. CHARLES sits in his place, next to FIONA. He puts his arm round her.

The service begins. The coffin is there, in the middle of the aisle. The local priest speaks.

> **PRIEST: Good morning. And a warm welcome to you all on this cold day. Our service will begin in a few minutes – but first, we have asked Matthew, Gareth's closest friend, to say a few words.**

MATTHEW, seated with the parents, steps forward. He takes a speech from his pocket.

MATTHEW: Gareth used to prefer funerals to weddings. He said it was easier to get enthusiastic about a ceremony one had an outside chance of eventually being involved in.

Everyone smiles, they are immediately at ease.

MATTHEW: In order to prepare this speech I rang a few people to get a general picture of how Gareth was regarded by those who met him. 'Fat' seems to have been a word people most connected with him. 'Terribly rude' also rang a lot of bells. So, 'very fat and very rude' seems to have been the stranger's viewpoint.

On the other hand, some of you have been kind enough to ring me, and let me know that you loved him – which I know he would have been thrilled to hear. You remember his fabulous hospitality, his strange, experimental cooking – the recipe for Duck à la Banana fortunately goes with him to his grave. Most of all, you tell me of his enormous capacity for joy and, when joyful, for highly vocal drunkenness. But I hope joyful is how you will remember him. Not stuck in a box in a church. Pick your favourite of his waistcoats and remember him that way: the most splendid,

replete, big-hearted, weak-hearted as it turned out, and jolly bugger most of us ever met.

As for me, you may ask how I will remember him, what I thought of him. Unfortunately, there I run out of words. Perhaps you will forgive me if I turn for my own feelings to the words of another splendid bugger, W. H. Auden...

At first he modestly reads it, and then looks up and speaks it, not consulting the paper in front of him.

MATTHEW: This is actually what I want to say:

'Stop all the clocks, cut off the telephone.
Prevent the dog from barking with a juicy bone.
Silence the pianos and with muffled drum
Bring out the coffin, let the mourners come.

Let aeroplanes circle moaning overhead
Scribbling on the sky the message He Is Dead,
Put the crêpe bows round the white necks of the
 public doves,
Let the traffic policemen wear black cotton gloves.

He was my North, my South, my East and West,
My working week and my Sunday rest,
My noon, my midnight, my talk, my song;
I thought that love would last for ever: I was wrong.

The stars are not wanted now; put out every one;
Pack up the moon and dismantle the sun;
Pour away the ocean and sweep up the wood;
For nothing now can ever come to any good.'

During the final verse we move outside, as the coffin is carried and put into the car. Behind the chapel is a huge factory. People move slowly back to their cars.

DAVID leaves CHARLES and walks away with SERENA. FIONA moves gently to SCARLETT.

CARRIE approaches CHARLES.

> CHARLES: Good of you to come – must have been the shortest honeymoon in history.
>
> CARRIE: No, it's fine. We'll do it some other time.

Pause: there are things to say.

> CARRIE: You know, that thing you said in the street...
>
> CHARLES: Yes, I'm sorry about that.
>
> CARRIE: No – I liked it. I liked you saying it.

A long pause before she kisses him on the cheek and walks away. He watches her go.

> FIONA: Charlie – I'll take Scarlett home.
>
> CHARLES: Darling Fi.

He kisses her goodbye. She walks away holding SCARLETT's hand – it is the first time we've seen them affectionate. CHARLES stands alone. TOM comes up behind.

> TOM: Walk, Charlie?
>
> CHARLES: Yes. That would be grand.

They begin to stride.

> TOM: Never felt like that – I mean, something vaguely similar for Jilly when I was young...

CHARLES: Jilly?

TOM: Labrador.

CHARLES: Yes – it's odd, isn't it – all these years we've been single and proud of it, we never noticed that two of us were to all intents and purposes married all the time.

TOM: Traitors in our midst.

CHARLES *smiles. They arrive by the river's edge. Bleak. Grey.*

TOM: In a way I think death is hardest for the parents, don't you? I hope I die before my children.

CHARLES: Tom – one thing I find really... (*Can't find the word*) is your total confidence that you will get married. What if you never find the right girl?

TOM: Sorry?

CHARLES: Surely if that service shows anything, it shows that there is such a thing as a perfect match. If we can't be like Gareth and Matthew, then maybe we should just let it go. Some of us are not going to get married.

TOM: Well, I don't know, Charlie. The truth is, unlike you, I never expected the thunderbolt – I always just hoped that I'd meet some nice, friendly girl, like the look of her, hope the look of me didn't make her physically sick – then pop the question and settle down and be happy. It worked for my parents...well, apart from the divorce and all that.

CHARLES: I give you six months at the outside, Tom. Yes, maybe you're right. (*Thinking it through*) Maybe all this waiting for one true love stuff gets you nowhere.

And an alarm clock rings.

JULY 15TH

81. INT. CHARLES'S BEDROOM. DAY.

The alarm still rings.

CHARLES *sleepily switches it off. He relaxes back. Then another alarm clock goes off. Then another. Then another…*

    CHARLES: **What the fuck is going on?**

He looks up. There are 10, 20, 30 alarm clocks spread around the room. He looks round, and TOM *– in bed with him – gets up.*

    TOM: **Thought we better make absolutely sure we weren't late.**

CHARLES *is confused and his hair is in the most total mess.*

TOM: Excellent wedding hairstyle, by the way.

CUT TO
A FINAL
INVITATION:

You are cordi
invited to attend the

Charles &

*St. Julian's, Smithfield,
London EC1*

82. INT. CHARLES & SCARLETT'S KITCHEN. DAY.

CHARLES *is still in his sleeping shorts and T-shirt.* MATTHEW *has arrived, wearing a bright tartan waistcoat and tails.*

CHARLES: Matthew – the best looking best man in the world. Listen – thank you for doing this today.

MATTHEW: Of course.

CHARLES *gives him a hug. It acknowledges that* MATTHEW's *life has not been easy these months.*

CHARLES: I wish Gareth was here.

MATTHEW: Bet he does too. Sorry we're so late. The others are just parking the car. I thought we'd all go with Tom.

CHARLES: Late? So late?

MATTHEW: Yes – it's 9.45.

CHARLES: 9.45?!

MATTHEW: Yup – forty-five minutes till 'I do'.

CHARLES: Bloody Tom! I told him to set the alarm for eight. O fucky fuck.

He charges out, passing SCARLETT *slouching in, just woken.*

MATTHEW: Scarlett?

SCARLETT: O – Hi.

MATTHEW: You ready?

SCARLETT: Absolutely. Give me twenty seconds.

She moves to put on a cup of coffee.

83. EXT. WEDDING 4 CHURCH. DAY.

TOM's *Land Rover skids into position outside the church.* CHARLES *shoots out, doing his tie as he runs.*

CHARLES: Time?

MATTHEW: Honestly?

CHARLES: Yes. Time?

MATTHEW: It's about ten to nine.

CHARLES *runs on – 5 seconds later it registers. He walks back to them, laughing in the car,* SCARLETT *taking his picture.*

CHARLES: Bastards.

84. INT. BEDROOM. THE BRIDE'S PARENTS' HOUSE. DAY.

A fantasy of flowers, petticoats, bridesmaids in dresses. We see a crown of flowers being perfected – but not the face of the bride who is going to wear it.

85. EXT. WEDDING 4 CHURCH. GRAVEYARD. DAY.

SCARLETT takes a snap of the friends all sitting in the graveyard – CHARLES, TOM, MATTHEW, FIONA, DAVID, SCARLETT and SERENA. They've been round the corner and got breakfast while waiting for the other guests – that's seven cappucinos and one full English breakfast for TOM.

> TOM: **This is splendid tuck!**

SCARLETT is in tails like the boys. FIONA is standing with a polystyrene tea-cup. She, usually in black and grey, is dressed in a bright, colourful jacket.

> FIONA: **Yes – I think I might say a little word.**
>
> SCARLETT: **Yeh!!!**
>
> FIONA: **As many of you know, I have been a close observer of Charles's love life for many years now – but recently I'd started to despair, and fear that really he was married to us lot – apart from the fact we won't have his babies.**
>
> TOM: **O, I don't know about that...**
>
> FIONA: **But fortunately, it's all turned out splendidly – the girl in question is, sadly, crazy – but perhaps that's why he loves her. So, I'd like to propose a toast to my Charlie and his beautiful girl on this tragic day. Be happy and don't forget us.**
>
> CHARLES: **Thank you.**
>
> FIONA: **To Charles...and Duckface.**
>
> ALL: **Charles and Duckface!**

They all toast him in coffee.

86. INT. BEDROOM. THE BRIDE'S PARENTS' HOUSE. DAY.

The crown of flowers that we have just seen being prepared is finally ready – it is carried – and laid on to the head of HENRIETTA.

> HENRIETTA: **What do you think?**
>
> HELENA: **You look divine.**
>
> HENRIETTA: **It does work, doesn't it. Yes.**

HENRIETTA *smiles*.

87. EXT. WEDDING 4 CHURCH. GRAVEYARD. DAY.

CHARLES *is replying on his own behalf.*

> CHARLES: **Well, I'd like to thank Fiona for those charming words about my future wife. And I'd like to take this opportunity before the day starts to read a little message from her to you all.**

He takes out a piece of paper.

TOM: This is exciting.

CHARLES: She says: 'Any of you come near my house, I'll set the dogs on you.'

TOM *finds this very funny.*

TOM: 'I'll set the dogs on you!'

88. EXT. WEDDING 4 CHURCH. DAY.

As they all walk to the church, there in front of them is John, whose wife had been fooling around with Toby de Lisle.

MATTHEW: Hi.

JOHN: I hope me damn sister turns up – not much of a wedding without a bride! Bit of a poor show you not having a stag night.

CHARLES: O but we did, we did, we did...n't think it was a very good idea in this day and age.

John: Really?

They move on quickly as John tries to work this out.

89. INT. WEDDING 4 CHURCH. DAY.

CHARLES *walks into the huge, still, empty church.* FIONA *joins him. Hands him an order of service.*

CHARLES: Fi – you do look lovely today.

FIONA: Yes, as you can see, I've abandoned my traditional black.

CHARLES: So you have.

FIONA: From now on, I shall be all the colours of the rainbow. Fall in love with someone who fancies me for a change.

CHARLES: Darling Fi.

She smiles – they kiss a friendly kiss, her red lipstick all over his cheek. FIONA wipes it off.

FIONA: O, that won't do at all, will it?

It is all all right. They've been through their own private little war.

90. EXT. WEDDING 4 CHURCH. DAY.

The guests start to arrive. Car doors opening, hats, shoes, coats.

91. INT. WEDDING 4 CHURCH. DAY.

CHARLES still pacing in the church. The vicar wishes him good luck.

92. EXT. WEDDING 4 CHURCH. DAY.

SCARLETT and MATTHEW receive guests outside. Suddenly she screams. She has spied her tall American – she rushes up to him and jumps up, with her legs around his waist.

SCARLETT: I thought you'd gone back to Texas.

CHESTER: Without you – never.

93. INT. WEDDING 4 CHURCH. DAY.

CHARLES inside, hands deep in his pockets.

94. INT. WEDDING 4 CHURCH. DAY.

Now inside the church, MATTHEW with CHARLES's old madman from the first reception.

> MATTHEW: *(Pause)* **Bride or groom?**
>
> OLD MADMAN: **It should be perfectly obvious I'm neither. Good God.**

95. INT. WEDDING 4 CHURCH. DAY.

TOM at the door with a sweet-looking, slightly awkward girl.

> TOM: **Bride or groom?**
>
> DEIRDRE: **Bride.**

He looks at her – it is a moment of total first love. Big pause.

> TOM: **Ahm, yes. Fine. You know, I've got a feeling we've met before.**
>
> DEIRDRE: **We have – about twenty-five years ago – I'm second cousin Harold's daughter, Deirdre. You're Tom.**
>
> TOM: **Good Lord. So you're family.**
>
> DEIRDRE: **Yes.**

Love is in their eyes.

> DEIRDRE: **Only very distant.**
>
> TOM: **Well, yes, of course.** *(Pause)* **You said you were... 'bride'?**
>
> DEIRDRE: **Yes.**
>
> TOM: **Well, do sit, do sit here, Deirdre.**

He walks away, dazed.

96. INT. WEDDING 4 CHURCH. DAY.

CHARLES *shaking hands.* LYDIA *and* BERNARD.

> CHARLES: How are you?
>
> BERNARD: Exhausted, actually.

LYDIA *grabs him and takes him away.* CHARLES *turns and suddenly there is* CARRIE, *coming in unaccompanied, very quietly and elegantly dressed.*

> CARRIE: Hi.
>
> CHARLES: Hi.
>
> CARRIE: You look lovely: but then, as you know, I always liked you dressed for weddings. And on time.

She smiles. So does he. They're happy with this.

> CHARLES: Yes. It's an extraordinary thing. (*Tiny pause*) How's Hamish?
>
> CARRIE: O he's fine... I believe.
>
> CHARLES: You believe?
>
> CARRIE: Yes. He wasn't the man for me after all.

CHARLES *is shocked.*

> CHARLES: You left him?
>
> CARRIE: We left each other.

He takes her aside. She's just a little precarious now.

> CHARLES: When?

CARRIE: O, a few months now. March was hell. By April, it was sorted. *(Trying to make light of it)* **That's absolutely the last time I marry someone three times my age.**

MATTHEW *interrupting – it's all 'go'.*

MATTHEW: **Charlie – Charles – time to travel...**

CHARLES: *(Distracted)* **Yes, yes...** *(then polite)* **Coming, good, good.** *(To* CARRIE*)* **So why didn't you get in touch then?**

CARRIE: **I did think about it. I wanted to...but I was in a state... So anyway – I don't want to keep you.**

She clearly has remembered him intensely. But she gathers herself.

CARRIE: **I'll see you afterwards.**

CHARLES: **Yes, fine, excellent.**

    CHARLES: Wait –

He may be about to say something very important – but no...

    CHARLES: I'll show you to your seat...

*They head into the body of the church together... Down the aisle...
Passing John.*

    CHARLES: I'm just showing her to her seat.

*They walk along in silence for a few seconds. They reach the end of the
pew – then, just before turning into it, they step aside.*

    CARRIE: Our timing's been really bad, hasn't it?

    CHARLES: It's been bad.

    CARRIE: It's been a disaster.

    CHARLES: It has, as you say, been very bad indeed. God, it's
    lovely to see you.

Pause. Love. But they know the situation. She brightens.

    CARRIE: Well, good luck. It's pretty easy – just say 'I do'
    whenever anyone asks you a question.

She walks away. CHARLES *stays.*

CUT TO: CHARLES *with* MATTHEW, *mid-aisle.*

    MATTHEW: Shall we leave the ushing to us ushers and take
    our positions up front?

    CHARLES: Ahm – could you just give me a sec, Matthew?

...It's clearly not all over.

    MATTHEW: Of course, freshen up at will.

97. INT. WEDDING 4 CHURCH. VESTRY. DAY.

CHARLES enters a side room. It is empty, very quiet and very ecclesiastical.

CHARLES: Dear Lord – forgive me for what I am about to say in this magnificent place of worship. Bugger! Bugger! Bugger! Bugger! Bugger! Bugger!

A very sweet-natured VERGER pops his head out from behind a curtain where he has been washing his hands.

VERGER: Can I help at all?

CHARLES: No, thanks. Sorry. Vocal exercises. Big church.

VERGER: Excellent – often do the same myself – not exactly the same vocab, obviously. Rather more 'halleluias'. I'll leave you.

98. EXT. WEDDING 4 CHURCH. DAY.

The big black car pulls up outside the church, and HENRIETTA steps out in full regalia, with her father.

99. INT. WEDDING 4 CHURCH. DAY.

Everyone is now seated – there is an air of expectation. MATTHEW moves to TOM.

MATTHEW: Bride's arriving.

TOM: O fabulous. We seem to have lost the groom.

MATTHEW: Ah – do you want to see if you can stall her – and I'll see if I can find him.

TOM: Roger. Wilko.

MATTHEW heads off purposefully.

100. INT. WEDDING 4 CHURCH. VESTRY. DAY.

MATTHEW *knocks and enters.* CHARLES *is leaning on a chair.*

>**MATTHEW:** Charles – good to see you.

CHARLES *looks round at him. He's not happy. Under big strain.*

>**CHARLES:** Matt – what do we think about marriage?

>**MATTHEW:** Gosh – ahm – well, I think it's really good. If you love the person with all your heart.

>**CHARLES:** Well exactly. Quite. All these weddings – all these years – all that blasted salmon and champagne, and here I am on my own wedding day, and I'm still thinking.

>**MATTHEW:** Can I ask about what?

>**CHARLES:** No. No, I think best not.

101. EXT. WEDDING 4 CHURCH. DAY.

TOM, *heading off* HENRIETTA *and her father, who are striding towards the church.*

>**TOM:** I'm terribly sorry – there's a bit of a delay: there's a slight problem with the flowers.

>**HENRIETTA:** Flowers? What?

>**TOM:** Unfortunately there seems to be a staggeringly high proportion of hay-fever sufferers in the congregation, and they've been stuck right next to the damn flowers, so we're just moving them – the congregation.

They keep walking at him.

>**TOM:** Don't want the damn vows to be obliterated by the sound of sneezing

102. INT. WEDDING 4 CHURCH. VESTRY. DAY.

DAVID *now in with* MATTHEW *and* CHARLES.

>MATTHEW: Charles...would it be out of place for me to say that time is ticking by?

DAVID *hits the table to get* CHARLES's *attention*.

>DAVID: *What's happening? Tell me.*

>CHARLES: *O God! I just saw Carrie and she's separated.*

>DAVID: *Charles. It's your wedding day...*

103. INT. WEDDING 4 CHURCH. DAY.

The congregation are getting edgy at the delay – FIONA, BERNARD. TOM *reports back to* SCARLETT.

>TOM: I think I've fooled them so far – the great advantage of having a reputation for being stupid – people are less suspicious of you.

104. INT. WEDDING 4 CHURCH. VESTRY. DAY.

>CHARLES: *What's your advice?*

>DAVID: *You've got three choices: one – go ahead with it.*

CHARLES *nods*.

>DAVID: *Second – go outside and say, 'Sorry folks, it's all off.'*

>CHARLES: *Not tempting. Next...*

>DAVID: *Third...*

CUT TO: CHARLES *waiting expectantly....*

DAVID: *I can't think of a third.*

CHARLES: *Damn.*

Suddenly there is a knock on the door – they're all terrified – 'Is it the bride?' is the fear.

MATTHEW: *(Calling out)* **Hello?**

The VICAR enters.

VICAR: **Ah – here you are – ready to face the enemy?**

MATTHEW: **Are we?**

They all look towards CHARLES.

CHARLES: **Yes. Excellent.**

105. INT. WEDDING 4 CHURCH. DAY.

Outside the door of the vestry. The door opens. They are all standing there – ready to face the fray. They walk together. CHARLES *just glimpses* CARRIE *– but heads on to his fate and take his place in the pew at the front.*

Cut to TOM *at the back of the church. The organ begins. He gives a thumbs up – everything is AOK for action.*

It is the Wedding March. CHARLES *and* MATTHEW *stand.*

The doors at the back open to reveal HENRIETTA *and her father. She looks proud and glowing as she walks down the aisle, her father by her side, holding her arm.*

CHARLES *steps into position in the aisle at the front.* HENRIETTA *continues to advance, with a small yank on her father's arm.*

HENRIETTA: **Not so tight, Dad.**

She arrives. The priest steps forward. CHARLES *smiles at him and her.*

> VICAR: Dearly beloved. We are gathered together here in the sight of God and in the face of this congregation to join together this man and this woman in holy Matrimony...

CUT TO: *All the friends, listening intently.*

> VICAR: Which is an honourable estate, instituted of God in the time of man's innocence, signifying unto us the mystical union that is betwixt Christ and his Church and therefore is not by any to be enterprized, nor taken in hand unadvisedly, lightly or wantonly...

Close up on CHARLES. *This is it.*

> VICAR: But reverently, discreetly, advisedly, soberly, and in the fear of God. Therefore, if any man can show any just cause why they may not lawfully be joined together, let him speak now, or else hereafter for ever hold his peace.

The usual pause. Settle on CHARLES. *And then there is a knocking from behind, knuckles on wood.*

CHARLES *and* HENRIETTA *turn – everyone looks for who it could be.*

> VICAR: I'm sorry – does someone have something to say?

CUT TO: DAVID, *who raises his hand. Cut between him and* CHARLES.

> VICAR: Yes – what is it?
>
> CHARLES: One second. (*He starts to sign*) **What's going on?**
>
> DAVID: *I thought of a third option.*
>
> CHARLES: *What?*
>
> DAVID: *Will you translate?*
>
> CHARLES: *Translate what?*
>
> VICAR: What's going on, Charles?

HENRIETTA: Charles – what?

CHARLES: He wants me to translate what he's saying.

VICAR: What is he saying?

CHARLES: He says...(*And he watches* DAVID) '*I suspect the groom is having doubts: I suspect the groom would like to delay. I suspect the groom... I suspect the groom...*

DAVID: ...*Really loves someone else. That's true, isn't it, Charles?*

CHARLES *doesn't sign back.*

DAVID: *Because, Charlie – this is for the rest of your life – finally, you've got to marry the person you love with your whole heart.*

CUT TO: CHARLES. *Then* DAVID *again.*

DAVID: *And by the way – your flies are undone.*

CHARLES *just does a tiny look down.*

VICAR: What's he saying?

CHARLES: He says, he suspects the groom loves someone else.

VICAR: And do you? Do you love someone else? Do you, Charles?

Pause.

Cut round everyone – HENRIETTA, ANGUS, LAURA, BERNARD, LYDIA, SCARLETT, TOM, HENRIETTA *again. Then, like someone saying his vows…*

CHARLES: I do.

Pause.

A fist enters frame and hits CHARLES. *It is* HENRIETTA's. *The camera follows him as he falls, then moves slowly high up into the church as below chaos reigns –* HENRIETTA *hasn't finished with him.*

Rain and thunder sound outside the kitchen.

SCARLETT: **Blimey.**

The friends are there – it is the aftermath.

TOM: *(Optimistically)* **At least it's one we won't forget. I
mean a lot of weddings just blend into each other, don't
they, but this is one that will really stick out in the memory.**

MATTHEW: **For not actually including a wedding service.**

This is the first time we see CHARLES *– he has a black eye. He sits at the
table.*

FIONA: **Poor girl. I mean it – poor girl. I mean she's not my
favourite person in the world, but I think that may have
been an unforgiveable thing you did today.**

CHARLES *is very shaken.*

CHARLES: **I can't bear to think about it.
Poor Hen.**

TOM: **Though, let's face facts – I mean,
if you weren't sure you wanted to marry
her today of all days, i.e. your wedding
day, it must be the right decision, must-
n't it?**

FIONA *turns to him to deliver her usual 'fuck off,
Tom' – then just brushes his cheek affectionately.*

FIONA: **Quite right, Tom.**

SCARLETT: **It's a lovely dress. I'm sure she'll find it useful
for parties.**

DAVID: *I blame myself.*

MATTHEW: **What did he say?**

CHARLES: He says he blames himself.

ALL: *(Simultaneously)* No, absolutely not/No, you mustn't...

CHARLES *looks up at* DAVID.

CHARLES: **They all blame you too.**

Pause. A doorbell rings. They all get up, all relieved to have an excuse to move.

CHARLES: **No, no. If there's music to be faced, I should be facing it.**

He walks out.

107. INT/EXT. DOORWAY. CHARLES & SCARLETT'S HOUSE. LATE AFTERNOON.

CHARLES *opens his door. There in front of him is* CARRIE *– very wet. It still pours with rain.*

CARRIE: **Hello.**

CHARLES: **Hi. You're soaking. Come in.**

CARRIE: **No, no, I'm fine. There comes a point when you're so wet, you can't get any wetter.**

CHARLES: **OK. I'll come out.**

He steps into the rain. Within seconds he is soaking too.

CARRIE: **No please, don't – I just wanted to check you were OK – not busy killing yourself or anything. But you're fine, so... I shouldn't have come to the church this morning. I'm sorry.**

She walks away. He follows her.

CHARLES: No – wait – it was all my fault – I'm the bastard here. And it definitely sorted out one thing – which is, marriage and me – we're very clearly not meant for one another. It sorted out another big thing as well – there I was standing there in the church and, for the first time in my whole life, I realised I totally and utterly loved one person – and it wasn't the person standing next to me in the veil… It's the person standing opposite me now… in the rain.

Pause. He's done it. At last he has said that he loves her.

CARRIE: Is it still raining? I hadn't noticed.

CHARLES: The truth of it is I've loved you from the first second I met you. You're not suddenly going to go away again, are you?

CARRIE: No, I might drown, but otherwise, no.

CHARLES: OK, OK – we'll go in.

Turns to take her in. They walk a few paces, but then…

CHARLES: First, let me ask you one thing. Do you think…

She watches him.

CHARLES: …after we've dried off, after we've spent lots of time together, you might agree…not to marry me? And do you think not being married to me might maybe be something you could consider doing for the rest of your life?

She looks at him.

CHARLES: Do you?

CARRIE: I do.

They kiss. The camera moves into the stormy skies above London and a thunderbolt lights the sky.

ALMOST THE END.

During the credits we see snapshots of the future. To the sound of 'Chapel of Love'.

HENRIETTA *and her perfectly matched boyfriend from the Guards in an avenue of raised sabres.*

DAVID *and* SERENA – *kissing and confetti.*

SCARLETT *and* CHESTER – *her in a big Texan hat,
him in a shiny waistcoat, outside a registry office,
kissing as two delighted old ladies watch on.*

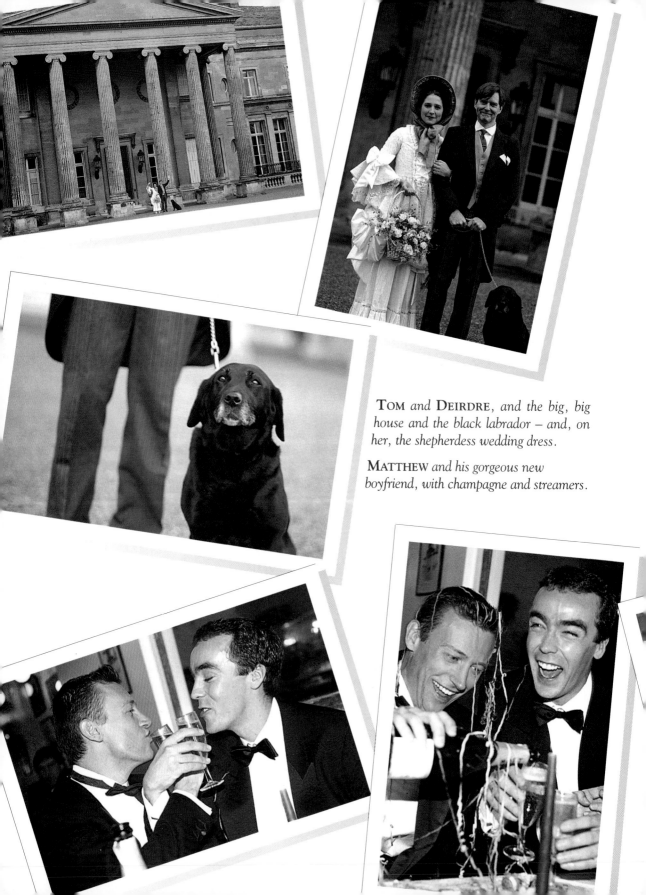

TOM and **DEIRDRE**, *and the big, big house and the black labrador – and, on her, the shepherdess wedding dress.*

MATTHEW *and his gorgeous new boyfriend, with champagne and streamers.*

FIONA, *gleeful next to her slightly sombre new beau, Prince Charles.*

And finally, CHARLES *and* CARRIE *and their little boy.*

The end

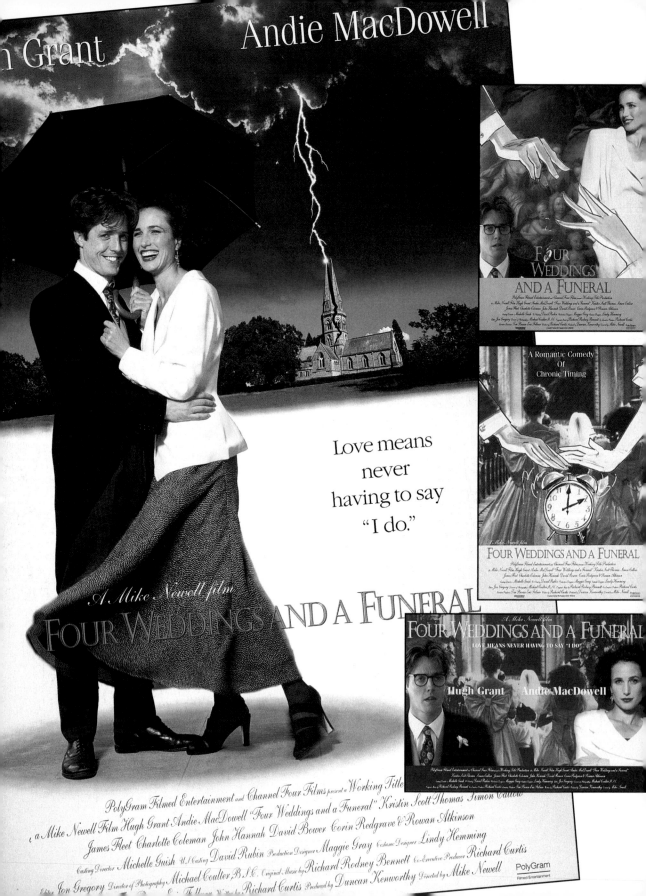

Appendix 1

THE POSTERS.

Particular thanks to Sam in America, and David and Chris over here for all their endless work on these.

Here are some of the posters that either were or might have been.

All of these are early drafts for the UK poster. We tried for a while to give the public a glimpse of Scarlett's turquoise underpants. We failed.

LOVE IS ALL AROUND

HUGH GRANT   ANDIE MacDOWELL

"SO SO FUNNY YOU'LL CRY WITH LAUGHTER"

DAILY EXPRESS

"MISS IT AT YOU PER

THE SU

NO.1 IN U.K, U.S.A EUROPE & AUSTRALIA

MAYBE WE DIDN'T MAKE THE WORLD CUP. BUT WE DID MAKE THE WORLD LAUGH.

A MIKE NEWELL FILM

four Weddings and a funeral 15

KRISTIN SCOTT THOMAS   SIMON CALLOW   JAMES FLEET   JOHN HANNAH   CHARLOTTE COLEMAN   DAVID BOWER   CORIN REDGRAVE AND ROWAN ATKINSON

PolyGram
Filmed Entertainment

▲The 2nd UK 'Pump-It-Up' poster.

HIDE and SEEK.

four Weddings and a funeral

CAT and MOUSE.

four Weddings and a funeral

four Weddings and a funeral

Sometimes Love beats you at your own game.

▲The first, rather radical, American idea.

▲ Korea's choice.

Japan goes for pink. ▼

▲ The actual poster from America.

▲ That catchy Korean logo again.

Appendix 2
TITLES & STRAP LINES.

a) TITLES

On the last film I wrote, we changed the title. It was called 'Camden Town Boy' – but then it was decided that no-one in New Jersey had heard of Camden Town. So after much faffing and taffing, it was called 'The Tall Guy'. Shame, I now think.

However, sure enough, as we neared the end of production, the same title crisis reared its head about the film so far called 'Four Weddings and a Funeral'. A fax came through from America saying there was a feeling that boys didn't like weddings and no-one liked funerals. The title suggested a film that everyone in the world would want to miss.

So the long search began. These are some of the twists and turns we went through just to decide on five words. First, the ones we and our Americans made up and then swiftly, quite swiftly, discarded:

TOFFS ON HEAT	TAKING THE PLUNGE
THE COURSE OF TRUE LOVE	EXCLUSIVE ENGAGEMENTS
LOITERING IN SACRED PLACES	FOOLS RUSH IN
CHAMPAGNE AND ASHES	ALL THE BLUSHING BRIDESMAIDS
CHARLES AND CHUMS	TIPTOE DOWN THE AISLE
IN LOVE IN ENGLAND	A HOLY MISERY *(eh?)*
MAKE YOUR MIND UP TIME	NUPTIALS AND NIGHTCAPS
ALWAYS LATE	THE SERIAL MONOGAMIST
TRUE LOVE AND DEATH	INVITING COMPANIONS
THE WHITES OF THEIR GOWNS	

This lot weren't much more popular:

SKULKING AROUND	STILL SINGLE AFTER ALL THESE YEARS
SINGLE AND PROUD OF IT	MARRIAGE BLUES

THE WEDDING SEASON	BACHELOR BLUES
WEDDINGS A GO GO	GIRLS IN BIG WHITE DRESSES
NOT TO BE TAKEN LIGHTLY	LOVE, DEATH AND CHAMPAGNE
ANY JUST CAUSE OR IMPEDIMENT	LOVE AND DEATH AND US
TAILCOATS AND CONFETTI	JUST SAY 'I DO'
SALMON AND CHAMPAGNE	THE BACHELOR
ALL THE BRIDES AND GROOMS	THE ETERNAL BACHELOR
EVERYONE'S GETTING MARRIED	ALWAYS THE BRIDESMAID
BUT NOT FOR ME	NEVER THE GROOM

And these were, to say the least, on the unimaginative side:

FOUR WEDDINGS, TWO FUCKS AND A FUNERAL
FOUR WEDDINGS, FIVE VICARS AND A FUNERAL
FOUR WEDDINGS, SEVEN FRIENDS AND A FUNERAL
FOUR WEDDINGS, NINE BRIDESMAIDS AND A FUNERAL
LOTS OF WEDDINGS, SOME SEX AND A FUNERAL

Finally we rejected all of these, and settled on this short list:

GOING TO THE CHAPEL
THE LAST BACHELOR
A TALE OF RINGS AND OTHER THINGS
FOUR WEDDINGS, A FUNERAL AND A CUP OF TEA
FOUR WEDDINGS, SOME SEX AND A FUNERAL

But when these didn't make the grade either, we finally settled on a choice of two. A fairly familiar one, and a startling new last-minute insider. The choice was between:

FOUR WEDDINGS AND A FUNERAL *and* THE BEST MAN.

We then remembered that 'The Best Man' is the name of an old Henry Fonda movie.

So we settled for the title on the front of this book. Though at our first night in London, Stephen Fry made a speech and christened it FWAAF (pronounced 'fwaf') – so that's really the title now.

b) STRAP LINES

FAX TO: Richard Curtis
FROM: Duncan Kenworthy
DATE: December 19 1993
RE: Strap Lines

Dear Richard

We need a smart copy line which somehow says that the film is very funny, very romantic, often stupid, sometimes sad, that Andie is wonderful, Hugh is divine, and there's this one great scene with a totally idiotic priest – five words maximum please.

Love Duncan.

We then spent months settling on that snappy line on the poster to capture the public's attention and affection. There were many, most of them dodgy. Here, just to give you a flavour, are eighteen:

FAX TO: Duncan Kenworthy
FROM: Richard Curtis
DATE: 19 January 1993
RE: Strap Lines

Dear Duncan

Help.

Love Richard.

P.S.

1. In Church No-one Can Hear You Scream.

2. A Love Story with a Message – Don't Get Married.

3. He's Had 9 Girlfriends. She's Had 33 Men.
Unfortunately, Practice Doesn't Make Perfect.

4. Love Means Never Having To Say 'I Do'.

5. Love Means Never Having To Say 'I'm Sorry – I Just Married Someone Else'.

6.   Four Weddings and a Funeral

            Or to be more accurate:

'4 Weddings, 1 Funeral, 4 Competent Priests, 1 Real Idiot, 6 Friends, 14 Bridesmaids, A Senile Relative, a Pair of Turquoise Underpants, Some Jokes, Some Noisy Sex and a Cup of Tea'

7. Would You Rather Get Married Or Get Buried? **Difficult call**.

8. GOVERNMENT WARNING – when you get married, it is advisable to love the person you are marrying. Do not, repeat, do not love someone else in the congregation more.

9. 4 Brides, 4 Grooms, 4 King funny.

10. 5 Sacred Occasions. 4 Total Cock-ups.

11. *(The Prince version)* Four Weddings and a Funeral.
4 every 1 who ever went 2 a wedding and 8 ted it.

12. Love and Marriage, Love and Marriage
Go Together Like a Horse and Cabbage.

13. Feel it in your fingers. Feel it in your Toes.
Love is all around you and so the Terror grows.

14. If Marriages are Made in Heaven – God Should be Sued for Shoddy Workmanship.

15. Going to Bed together – very easy.
Going down the Aisle together – very hard.

16. Not a good Advertisment for the State of Holy Matrimony (Not a bad Advertisment for True Love).

17. Very funny, Very romantic, ~~Very religious.~~

18. In the name of the Father, the Son and the Holy Goat. Amen.

c) THE TRAILERS

Just before the end of the filming, we got permission from Polygram to film a special trailer. In the end, we made another one after filming using lots of clips from the film, and the slogan – 'Four Weddings and a Funeral – A Film with a Message – Don't Get Married'. But here are the four trailers you almost saw:

TRAILER 1.

ANDIE *is talking straight to camera.*

ANDIE: Hi. My name is Andie MacDowell. I've just made a film in Britain called Four Weddings and a Funeral – it's real garbage...

MIKE (*Voice Over*): CUT! (*good natured*) Surely that's the wrong line, isn't it, Andie?

ANDIE: Yes – sorry. I'll try again.

MIKE (*V/O*): OK, keep running. And action...

ANDIE: Hi. My Name is Andie MacDowell. I've just made a film in Britain called Four Weddings and a Funeral – it's real good and real funny and I think it's going to be a real big failure at the Box Office.

MIKE (*V/O*): CUT!

ANDIE: I'm sorry, Mike. I got confused. One last time.

MIKE (*V/O*): OK – action!

ANDIE: Hi. My name is Julia Roberts. O shoot and doggone.

CAPTION: FOUR WEDDINGS AND A FUNERAL. COMING THIS SPRING. MUCH BETTER MADE THAN THE TRAILER.

TRAILER 2.

ANDIE *in a wedding dress.*

> ANDIE: Hi. My name is Andie MacDowell and not long from now I'm appearing in a film called Four Weddings and a Funeral, which is a film about four weddings and a funeral. This is one of the costumes from the film: it comes from the one of the weddings – not from the funeral. It would be real stupid to go to a funeral dressed in this sort of clothes. Unless you were crazy. In which case it would be a very reasonable way to behave. Also in the film is Hugh Grant.

The shot widens to reveal HUGH, *also in a wedding dress.*

> ANDIE: He doesn't wear this costume in any of the film. He just thought he'd wear it in the trailer. He's a bit like that.

TRAILER 3.

> CAPTION ON BLACK: ANDIE MACDOWELL.

CUT TO: ANDIE, *in a corner of a room, in confessing-to-psychiatrist style.*

> ANDIE: I went to England, and, ahm, I didn't know what to expect. I mean I'd read the script and I thought it was real funny – but I didn't know if there'd be any chemistry with Hugh, my co-star...

> CAPTION: HUGH GRANT.

HUGH *is sitting in the corner of another room. We cut between the two of them for the rest of the trailer.*

> HUGH: The second I met her I fell totally, maddeningly in love.

> ANDIE: I think there's chemistry on screen – but in real life – not really. Of course, it would have been nice if he'd been a bit friendlier during the filming...

> HUGH: The whole shoot was torture – every minute of every day I was afraid I'd just blurt out how much I adored her – so I just kept my distance.

> ANDIE: But that's it with movies – you can't expect to make friends every time, can you? Hugh just had other things on his mind.

> HUGH: I've left my wife and children – I live alone now.

> ANDIE: We'll probably exchange Christmas cards.

> HUGH: I've got seventeen hundred pictures of her in my bedroom.

> ANDIE: Yes, overall it was a happy experience, and the film is really great, real funny. I think you'll like it.

> HUGH: I wish I'd never heard of the damn film – I don't care if it's a hit – it ruined my life.

TRAILER 4.

We actually shot this one – but it didn't make it into the cinema. It was shown just once, on the Big Breakfast.

ANDIE *and* HUGH *hanging around informally on the set.*

> ANDIE: Hi. My name is Andie MacDowell – and I've just finished making a really great film in England called Four Weddings and a Funeral.

Pull back to reveal HUGH.

> ANDIE: My co-star is a really lovely guy, real handsome, real talented and now a really good friend – he's called...ahm...

HUGH *whispers his name.*

> ANDIE: Hugh. That's right. Hugh...ahm.(*Searching for his surname*)

HUGH *whispers again.*

> ANDIE: Grant. Hugh Grant. I'm an enormous fan of his and I've loved everything he's done, things like... (HUGH *whispers – but they mean nothing to her*) well, things like Four Weddings and a Funeral. Anyway...he's in it – and it's very funny and it's about four weddings and a funeral. Anything you want to say, Harry...

> HUGH: Hugh.

> ANDIE: Hugh – sorry, honey. I love this guy. Anything you want to say?

> HUGH: Well yes – do watch this film – it's about two people who love one another so much...they actually remember each other's names – it's very moving.

They sort of break into real informality.

> ANDIE: I'm sorry about that. I'm terrible with names. I had the same trouble with Bert Murray.

> HUGH: Bill Murray.

> ANDIE: That's the guy. And George.

> HUGH: That's George Depardieu?

> ANDIE: Right.

> CAPTION: FOUR WEDDINGS AND A FUNERAL. COMING THIS SPRING. REMEMBER THE TITLE, ANDIE WON'T.

Appendix 3

Scenes from the Cutting Room Floor – and some that didn't made it that far, for all sorts of reasons.

THE MADMAN.

This scene patently didn't belong in the film – I suppose it was my tribute to 'An American Werewolf in London'.

EXT. COUNTRY LANE. NIGHT.

CUT TO: CHARLES, *standing outside the Land Rover, in the middle of the road, in the middle of the night, in the middle of nowhere.*

> SCARLETT: **Be careful.**
>
> CHARLES: **Yes. If I'm found hacked into pieces in seven counties, tell the police it's not suicide.**
>
> SCARLETT: **All right – absolutely.**

As the car drives away – the friends start to shout the chorus of 'Can't Smile Without You'.

CUT TO: CHARLES *in a car with a man with a heavy regional accent. Complete contrast of the noisy friends' car to the chilly total silence here.*

MAN IN CAR: You from round these parts?

CHARLES: No, I live in London.

MAN IN CAR: O dear.

CHARLES: Have you been to London?

MAN IN CAR: What, and get mugged? No, thank you.

CHARLES: Not everyone who goes to London gets mugged you know.

MAN IN CAR: No, I suppose not. There's some as get raped. *(Pause)* Shouldn't be round these roads late at night you know.

CHARLES: Why's that?

MAN IN CAR: Maniacs.

CHARLES: Ah. Lots of them about, are there?

MAN IN CAR: So they say. That's why the heather grows so well.

CHARLES: How's that?

MAN IN CAR: Human blood's a very good fertiliser.

CHARLES: *(Getting concerned)* Ah.

MAN IN CAR: Few years ago, a young man like you disappeared. Chopped into seven pieces. They never found any of them.

CHARLES: Really? *(Worried pause)* How do you know about them then?

MAN IN CAR: What?

CHARLES: Well, if they never found any of them, how do you know about the seven pieces?

Man in car turns around and looks at CHARLES *very carefully.*

CHARLES: I wish I hadn't asked that.

Charles looks a little nervous. Checks his watch. He may have made a very unwise choice here.

ANOTHER SEDUCTION.

I wrote five versions of this scene in one day – and then we picked our favourite. This one came second.

INT. THE LUCKY BOATMAN PUB. NIGHT.

CHARLES *and* CARRIE *move from the landing into her bedroom.*

CARRIE: So how long do you think you have to talk to someone before sleeping with them has real meaning, rather than just being some tacky physical thing?

CHARLES: I don't know. Usually for me, it's about three weeks.

CARRIE: Perhaps we could rush it. What's Week One?

CHARLES: First week, we'd talk about the wedding because it was all we had in common.

CARRIE: Fine – what did we make of the wedding?

CHARLES: Dull, I thought.

CARRIE: Me too. Second week.

CHARLES: I suppose in the second week, we'd tell each other about ourselves.

CARRIE: I'm American, twenty-nine and my legs are a little short in comparison to the rest of my body.

CHARLES: And I'm English and my father's only got four fingers on his right hand.

CARRIE: Great, that's that sorted out. What happens in Week Three?

CHARLES: Week Three, I'd dither around a lot and ask you out for dinner, and then be awkward on your doorstep three times, and then finally get round to popping the question...

CARRIE: What question is that?

CHARLES: Ahm – are most Americans worried about the constitutional deadlock between the Senate and the President?

She looks at him and laughs.

CUT TO: CHARLES and CARRIE making love. After thirty seconds...

CARRIE: No – they worry more about the breakdown of law and order in the inner cities.

FATHER-IN-LAWS AND OTHERS.

We actually shot most of this sequence, and the father-in-laws section, featuring the wonderful Jeremy Kemp and Robert Laing, worked very well. The problem was that it came right after Rowan's scene in the church – and when we watched the rough-cut, it suddenly felt like the movie was turning into a joke movie, and that we were losing touch with Charles's story. So, some things had to go.

INT. THE HOLBEIN HOTEL. CORRIDOR. DAY.

In the corridor there is a table where people put their gifts. George, the bore from the Boatman, approaches the table with a huge present, beautifully wrapped. He puts it down and heads to join the line. Next, GARETH and CHARLES sweep in.

> GARETH: Excuse me.

GARETH puts down a very small, unimpressive-looking gift. He inspects the other gifts, looks around to check no-one is watching, and swaps the card on his with George's present. He rejoins CHARLES, smiles happily and they head to the ballroom.

INT. THE HOLBEIN HOTEL. RECEPTION ROOM. DAY.

The front of the receiving line. A MASTER OF CEREMONIES dips his head and has a word with every guest, very discreetly...

> MASTER OF CEREMONIES: I think you should know that Lord Hibbott is a little deaf, sir.
>
> MATTHEW: O thank you.

He moves on – and after shaking hands with the wife, gets to the first father, SIR JOHN DELANEY.

> MATTHEW: *(Very loud)* EXCELLENT WEDDING – I WAS IN HEAVEN.
>
> SIR JOHN: I'm delighted.

MATTHEW moves on, and FIONA approaches Sir John – also shouting.

> FIONA: THE BRIDE LOOKED STUNNING! YOU MUST BE VERY PROUD!
>
> SIR JOHN: Yes, I am. *(He leans across to his wife)* Why is everybody shouting at me?

CUT TO: MATTHEW *talking to the next father.*

> MATTHEW: I thought the church looked exquisite.
>
> LORD HIBBOTT: Didn't she? Beautiful tiara I thought.
>
> MATTHEW: *(Worried)* Yes.

MATTHEW moves on. LORD HIBBOTT looks angrily down the line at the MASTER OF CEREMONIES. FIONA approaches.

FIONA: I thought your son looked very handsome.

LORD HIBBOTT: *(Worried but trying hard)* Yes, I believe the prawns are delicious.

Meanwhile GARETH *approaches the exasperated first father.*

GARETH: BRAVO – AN ABSOLUTELY SPLENDID OCCASION ALL ROUND!!!

SIR JOHN: *(Fuming)* Thank you.

FATHER GERALD: LOVELY WEDDING! EXQUISITE FLOWERS IN THE CHURCH!!!!

SIR JOHN: *(Shouting)* FOR HEAVEN'S SAKE, WHY IS EVERYBODY SHOUTING AT ME? I CAN HEAR PERFECTLY WELL!

FATHER GERALD: *(Still shouting)* SORRY!!!

CHARLES *is next. He smiles broadly.*

CHARLES: This is an excellent wedding.

TEN YEAR OLD LADY JANE: Where do you fit in?

NINE YEAR OLD RIGHT HONOURABLE HARRY: I'm the groom's brother. You?

LADY JANE: I'm the bride's cousin.

HON. HARRY: O. When I was little, I went into Bernard's bedroom, and he was pushing his willy into another boy.

LADY JANE: O, I'd better tell Lydia. She said she wanted to know everything about Bernard.

CUT TO: FATHER GERALD *who is talking to* SCARLETT.

SCARLETT: No, you were great.

FATHER GERALD: Did you think so? I thought I might have cocked it up a little.

SCARLETT: Well, now you say it, you did totally – but don't worry – I'm usually bored out of my box, but this time I really enjoyed it.

Pause.

SCARLETT: What do you think of the outfit?

FATHER GERALD: Nice. Nice.

SCARLETT: I don't think I should have gone for crimson. Not the dress – the pants underneath. I think crimson's a bit aggressive – you don't want to slip off a girl's dress and get punched in the face by a pair of crimson pants.

CUT TO: CHARLES: *He's talking to a very pretty woman – getting on famously.*

We didn't shoot this scene – but it was the section with which we auditioned all the people who might have played Charles. I suspect it may turn up in something else sometime, and it was probably because it was the type of scene that might pop up in something else sometime that it was cut.

CHARLES: ...Been to seven weddings this summer.

PRETTY WOMAN: You must get tired of champagne and salmon.

CHARLES: Yes, catering's always the problem. The last one I went to, the sister had done it. Unbelievable – though at least one knew who to lie to.

PRETTY WOMAN: Yes.

CHARLES: It just seems as though it's impossible to get it right. I mean, taste this: it's meant to be – what – pigeon: may be right actually – could be pigeon droppings. The asparagus looks and tastes like a Martian's penis, and the summer pudding was clearly made in late autumn, and left to die. Now, tell me, what do you do?

PRETTY WOMAN: I'm a caterer.

CHARLES: Good Lord – so you know what I'm talking about. Do you ever do weddings?

PRETTY WOMAN: Yes.

CHARLES: They should have asked you to do this one.

PRETTY WOMAN: They did.

CHARLES: God – I wish you hadn't turned it down.

PRETTY WOMAN: I didn't.

Long pause

CHARLES: Excellent. Excellent. If you'll just excuse me a moment, I think this knife should be sharp enough for the de-testiculation process.

SCARLETT AND GERALD: THE CONCLUSION.

INT. HOLBEIN HOTEL. RECEPTION. NIGHT.

SCARLETT, *much later, not very sober, still in conversation with* FATHER GERALD.

SCARLETT: Just checking: your kind of vicar – I know you can't get married, but how do things stand vis à vis just sort of, you know, sex in general, I mean, are you allowed to?

FATHER GERALD: Not really.

SCARLETT: O bad luck. Still – worth asking eh? Just in case.

CHARLES'S LIST.

This was the original continuation of the café scene – of which we shot about two thirds. But even that finally went under the knife .

CARRIE has just given CHARLES the list of all the men she's slept with.

>CARRIE: So there we go – less than Madonna – more than Princess Di – I hope. How about you – how many girls have you slept with?

>CHARLES: O God, ahm, well, nothing like that many. I don't know what the fuck I've been doing with my time actually. Work probably – that's it. Work.

>CARRIE: Well, go on.

>CHARLES: Ahm, well, let's see –

He counts on his fingers – 1, 2, 3. Pause. 4th Finger. Long pause.

>CHARLES: O, it must be about twenty.

>CARRIE: No, go on, try harder.

>CHARLES: *(He just can't come up with the numbers)* Five...six...all right, about fifteen.

>CARRIE: My husband says he's slept with eighty-four.

>CHARLES: That's a lie – he's lying. He's a filthy liar.

>CARRIE: Apparently not. He says the late Seventies were a very good period.

>CHARLES: Were they? The late Seventies – what the fuck was I doing then – listening to Abba when I could have been out shagging. Damn. That bastard Dancing Queen.

There is one of those moments when both sides just stop talking. Charles watches her sipping tea, and sort of smiles. Something's happened. She has a bite of cake – then looks at him – he snaps out of it.

>CHARLES: Sorry – sorry. *(Pause)* I wish I'd rung you. *(She smiles)* But then you didn't ring me either. You ruthlessly slept with me twice, and then never rang me.

>CARRIE: I wrote to you.

>CHARLES: When?

He is horrified – is this a lost letter tragedy?

>CARRIE: I sent you my wedding invitation.

>CHARLES: O yes, right. right...

CARRIE: What about you? You are so cute, I can't believe you haven't had some marriage offers.

CHARLES: Well, yes – Scarlett once offered to marry me in lieu of rent.

CARRIE: You're not tempted.

CHARLES: Not yet.

BROTHERS IN ADVERSITY.

This scene wasn't shot – but originally came after Charles's sort-of-confession of his love to Carrie on the Embankment.

EXT. WATERLOO BRIDGE. EVENING.

Charles and David look right along the Thames, with the lights of the city shining – darkness – total silence. They speak in sign.

CHARLES: *The thing I particularly like about being with you, David, is that we can talk to buggery without destroying the silence.*

DAVID: *Thank you.*

CHARLES: *Was that it? Was that true love? Was that the thing I've been waiting for for thirty-five years?*

DAVID: *Could be.*

CHARLES: *In which case, I've fucked up.*

DAVID: *Less your fault than a definitive example of bad timing.*

CHARLES: *Falling in love with someone three days before they get married.*

DAVID: *Yup. It's visiting relatives in Hiroshima on the day they drop the bomb.*

CHARLES: *It's meeting Lady Diana the afternoon she bumps into Prince Charles.*

DAVID: *It's dropping by for lunch with Jesus on Good Friday.*

CARRIE'S OTHER SPEECH.

An alternative draft of Carrie's wedding speech. For anyone who doesn't know him, I strongly recommend Jim Croce's Greatest Hits.

CARRIE *steps onto the little stage in the corner of the hall – there is much clapping.*

> CARRIE: The reason girls normally don't make speeches is that their Dads talk so much nonsense about how great they are, they dare not open their mouths in case they reveal the truth. Well, I'll take the risk, and just thank my father for not even mentioning my abortions and long stretches in various excellent women's prisons.

Others laugh. CHARLES *looks at her in wonder. And catches* SCARLETT's *eye. She pulls a face that says ' Well fancy that' – she actually believes the joke.*

> CARRIE: I only want to say two things. First, I love all of you here. O, except one close friend's new boyfriend, who stinks, but I haven't told her yet, and I'm sure this isn't the moment.

Cut round four worried men.

> CARRIE: And second, I just want to say that I love my husband with all my heart. I promise to love, serve and obey him for all our lives, on the condition that he does exactly the same for me, with perhaps just a little bit extra, because today it's so obvious I'm prettier than he is.

TOM *is loving this speech – massively impressed.*

> CARRIE: Jim Croce once said, 'I've looked around enough to know, you're the one I want to go through time with.' Well, I've looked around – and in some rather grim corners I'd rather forget – (you know who you are) – but now, I do know.

CLEVER CHILDREN.

INT. SCOTTISH WEDDING RECEPTION. NIGHT.

CUT TO: CHARLES – *and these two clever American kids in earshot.*

> KID 1: Pretty good service, I thought.

> KID 2: Yes – though as far as I can see having a wedding without mentioning divorce is like sending someone to war without mentioning that people are going to get killed.

> KID 1: Point. Did you enjoy the service?

STUPID ADULT: O, it was great – jolly pretty flowers, weren't they?

The kids look at each other in despair.

BROTHERS.

INT. BATHROOM. CHARLES & SCARLETT'S HOUSE. MORNING.

It is the morning of CHARLES's *wedding.* DAVID *and* CHARLES.

> CHARLES: *David – you know about this best man thing…*

DAVID *mimes a yawn.*

> CHARLES: *You really are my best man…*
>
> DAVID: *Thanks – but I would have made a really crap speech… I wouldn't marry you.*

CHARLES *looks at himself again.*

> CHARLES: *Nope. You're right. Not unless you were blind too.*
>
> DAVID: *I seriously thought I'd never see the day.*
>
> CHARLES: *Me neither.*

And then a moment of stillness between them – to register the special feeling of closeness…

> DAVID: *You said you'd never marry anyone except Debbie Harry.*
>
> CHARLES: *Unless Julie Andrews asked me nicely.*
>
> DAVID: *Life is full of bitter betrayals. I hope you'll be happy, Charlie.*

Appendix 4

BAD LANGUAGE: A NASTY STORY.

WARNING – don't read this at all if you liked the film in spite of the swearing. And whoever you are – don't read this all at once: it'll give you a slightly nauseous feeling, so just take it in bits.

SWEAR WORDS: THE PROBLEM

Quite near the start of filming, we discovered that contractually we had to produce a version of the film that would be suitable to be shown on Network American TV. This presented certain linguistic problems. Two months before the cameras rolled, we received a fax from Polygram in America – these are some of its highlights…

FAX TO: Working Title.
FROM: Mark Wolfe.
DATE: April 26, 1993.
RE: 'Four Weddings and a Funeral.'

1) LANGUAGE: Any use of the word 'fuck' is forbidden on television. More acceptable expletives are 'frig' (which is often used as it fits well in dubbing) or lesser words like 'damn'. Please try to avoid close-ups that clearly show the character saying 'fuck' as even looping in a new word will not do if the lip-read clearly says 'fuck'.

The jury is still out on 'shagging' and 'fag'. I would guess 'fag' will be a problem as it not only refers in the script to sex with young boys, but also because 'fag' is considered an offensive term for homosexuals. Fag does not mean a cigarette here.

'Nothing more off-putting at a wedding than a priest with an enormous erection'. That's a tough call. 'Enormous erection' alone is very questionable, but a priest having one is even worse. I doubt it'll fly on TV.

'Total penises'. That has two inherent problems. One, of course, is the word itself will not make it on TV (used as it is; used as a medical reference would be OK). The second problem is the fact that David and Charles sign it, therefore it would actually be *written* on the screen.

2) VISUAL: As I mentioned, we are repressed sexually here. On Network television you can not show:

Breasts, buttocks, lower frontal nudity of any gender; 'excessive thrusting' and screaming orgasms are not permitted.

3) SUBTITLES AND SIGN LANGUAGE: This film presents a unique problem. David and Charles cannot sign 'I'm fucked'. The subtitle obviously could not be shown, but also the actual signing should not read 'fuck'. It is not likely that the Networks would know sign language, but it wouldn't be allowed.

Well now, wasn't that fun. If you stick to these guidelines it'll make it a lot easier to sell to US TV. I ought to warn you that US Airlines are even worse.

I'm going to ask Mark to write my next script. By the way – the reference to 'fag' is because George, who drinks whisky with Charles in The Lucky Boatman, used to say **'I was at school with his brother Bufty. Tremendous bloke. I was his fag. Buggered me senseless – still, taught me a thing or two about life.'** *He doesn't anymore – to everyone's relief.*

SWEAR WORDS: THE SOLUTION

And so I set to work trying to replace everything which could be construed as in any way worrying to the most respectable of American matrons. It was an impossible task. But here is the document that finally went to Working Title to try out on our American partners.

FAX TO:	Working Title
FROM:	Richard Curtis
DATE:	3rd June 1993
RE:	Filthy Language in 'Four Weddings And A Funeral'

Dear All

Mark is right of course. The script is an offence to God and man – will any of these do?

love Richard

SCENE 11.

CHARLES: O fuck.

REPLACE WITH: O bugger.

I do worry that if the Americans don't know what **bugger** means all this won't be even the slightest bit funny to them. Please also check: **damn, buggeration, O God, Sod it, bastard, I don't believe it.**

SCENE 12.

SCARLETT: O fuck.

REPLACE WITH: O bugger.

SCENE 13.

CHARLES: Fuck.

REPLACE WITH: Bugger.

SCENE 14.

CHARLES: Fuck, we'll have to take yours.

REPLACE WITH: Bugger, we'll have to take yours.

SCENE 16.

CHARLES: Fuck it.

REPLACE WITH: Bugger it.

SCENE 17.

CHARLES: Fuck, fuck, fuckity, fuck.

REPLACE WITH: Buggeration!

SCENE 20.

CHARLES: Fiona – you're looking fucking beautiful – I couldn't tell you in church because of the 'fucking' bit.

CHARLES: ...Fucking beautiful.

Still haven't decided – something like **orgasm-inducingly**.

Please check: **sodding beautiful/wet-dreamily beautiful/groin-achingly/ball-breakingly beautiful**.

SCENE 22.

SCARLETT: ...She looked unbe-fucking-lievably pretty.

Please check: **unbe-bloody-lievably/unbe-sodding-lievably pretty/mouth-wateringly sexy...**

SCENE 23.

> CHARLES: **Bastard.**

I'm assuming all our bastards are all right. Whatever – think this one should remain. If not, try **swine, pig, damn, turd**.

> CHARLES: **...shagging...** (needs changing for its mis-meaning – in America it's a rather sweet old-fashioned dance. In USA, there'd be no harm in Charles revealing John's wife was 'shagging' Toby de Lisle)

Replace with **having it off/bonking/humping** – I'll ask Hugh which he likes.

SCENE 24.

> GARETH: **I would rather eat my grandfather's testicles.**

Please check whether it's all right – then try **grandmother's cholostomy bag**.

SCENE 31.

> GEORGE: **I was at school with his brother Bufty. Tremendous bloke. I was his fag. Buggered me senseless – still taught me a thing or two about life.**

> REPLACE WITH: **I was at school with his brother Bufty. Tremendous bloke. Thrashed me till my bottom turned blue – taught me everything I know about life.**

SCENE 37.

> CHARLES/SCARLETT: **O fuck/fuck...**

> REPLACE WITH: **O bugger/bugger.**

> SCARLETT: **All very well for you – I'm a fucking bridesmaid.**

> REPLACE WITH: **I'm a buggering bridesmaid.**

SCENE 45.

> LITTLE BOY: **...I saw Bernard pushing his willie into another boy.**

Please check: **...I saw him spanking a girl who didn't have any clothes on/ She must have been very naughty. I suppose so.** (ALTERNATIVE: Lydia was in bed with two chaps who didn't have any clothes on. And one of them was Cousin George)

> FATHER GERALD: **I think I may have cocked it up rather.**

> REPLACE WITH: **Ballsed it up/bished it up a bit/made a bit of a bish of it.**

SCENE 50.

> DAVID: *Did you really pork Miss Piggy?*

Is **pork** allowed – especially in the context of Miss Piggy?

SCENE 56.

SCARLETT: ...They just shag me and leave me.

REPLACE WITH: **Have sex with me/bonk me.** (I'll ask Charlotte)

SCENE 65.

CHARLES: **There's nothing more off-putting than a priest with an enormous erection.**

Please check – **You may be right though – there's nothing more off-putting than a sexually excited vicar.** Frankly, it seems such a moral minefield, I'd cut the whole line in America.

SCENE 66.

CHARLES: **What the fuck I've been doing with my time.**

REPLACE WITH: **What the hell/What in the name of buggery.**

SCENE 67.

DAVID: **'Penis' – in a non-medical context!**

Try **turd** – or is that only acceptable in a medical context too? **O Christ** – probably just cut it.

SCENE 71.

CHARLES: **Fuck-a-doodle-doo.**

Who can say? Might try **bugger-ugger-ugger it.** Except it sounds AWFUL.

SCENE 74.

FIONA: **Fuck off, Tom.**

Try with Kristen's voice: **Sod off, Tom/Bugger off, Tom.**

SCENE 97.

CHARLES: **Bugger, bugger, bugger, bugger, bugger.**

Try – **I absolutely totally and utterly do not sodding believe it.**

We made decisions on all of these – and every single swear word was either replaced before filming, or double shot during the filming.

The irony is that I believe the process brought more swearing into the world than it eradicated: every single time we finished a complicated shot and reminded Mike that he had to do it again for the American TV version, his reaction was definitely not 'O bugger'.

 Cast

(ALMOST IN ORDER OF APPEARANCE)

 Wedding 1

Charles	HUGH GRANT
Tom	JAMES FLEET
Gareth	SIMON CALLOW
Matthew	JOHN HANNAH
Fiona	KRISTIN SCOTT THOMAS
David	DAVID BOWER
Scarlett	CHARLOTTE COLEMAN
Carrie	ANDIE MACDOWELL
Angus the Groom	TIMOTHY WALKER
Laura the Bride	SARA CROWE
Vicar	RONALD HERDMAN
Laura's Mother	ELSPET GRAY
Laura's Father	PHILIP VOSS
George the Bore at the Boatman	RUPERT VANSITTART
Frightful Folk Duo	NICOLA WALKER
	PAUL STACEY
John with the Unfaithful Wife	SIMON KUNZ
Father Gerald	ROWAN ATKINSON
Serena	ROBIN McCAFFREY
The Boatman Waiter	MICHAEL MEARS
with	
Mad Old Man	KENNETH GRIFFITH

Wedding 2

Bernard the Groom	DAVID HAIG
Lydia the Bride	SOPHIE THOMPSON
Hamish	CORIN REDGRAVE
Master of Ceremonies	DONALD WEEDON
Tea-tasting Alistair	NIGEL HASTINGS
Vomiting Veronica	EMILY MORGAN
Naughty Nicki	AMANDA MEALING
Mocking Martha	MELISSA KNATCHBULL
Miss Piggy	POLLY KEMP

Henrietta	ANNA CHANCELLOR
Young Bridesmaid	HANNAH TAYLOR GORDON
Shop Assistant	BERNICE STEGERS
With	
Lord Hibbott	ROBERT LANG
Sir John Delaney	JEREMY KEMP
Mrs Beaumont	ROSALIE CRUTCHLEY

Wedding 3

Vicar	KEN DRURY
Best Man	STRUAN RODGER
Married Woman	LUCY HORNACK
Gorgeous Chester	RANDALL PAUL
Gareth's Dancing Partner	PAT STARR
Doctor	TIM THOMAS

A Funeral

Vicar	NEVILLE PHILLIPS

Wedding 4

Deirdre	SUSANNA HAMNETT
Polite Verger	JOHN ABBOTT
Vicar	RICHARD BUTLER

CREW

Production Supervisor	MARY RICHARDS
1st Assistant Director	KIERON PHIPPS
Production Sound Mixer	DAVID STEPHENSON
Location Manager	PAUL SHERSBY
Production Accountant	MICHELE TANDY
Chief Make-up & Hair Designer	ANN BUCHANAN
Camera Operator	PHILIP SINDALL
Focus Puller	CHRIS PLEVIN
Clapper Loader	MARK MILSOME
Camera Grip	RICHARD BROOME
2nd Camera Operator	JEREMY GEE
2nd Camera Assistant	SIMON FINNEY
2nd Camera Grip	MALCOLM SMITH
Camera Trainee	PETER HOWARD
Boom Operator	NICK FLOWERS
Sound Maintainance	GERRY BATES
Script Supervisor	JULIE ROBINSON
Script Editor	EMMA FREUD
Production Co-ordinator	PATSY de LORD
2nd Assistant Director	TREVOR PUCKLE
Co-2nd Assistant Director	PETER FREEMAN
3rd Assistant Director	OSCAR BEUSELINCK
Assistant Location Manager	CHRISTIAN McWILLIAMS
Assistant Accountant	DIANE CHRISTIAN
Cashier	MARILYN GOLDSWORTHY
1st Assistant Editor	IAN SEYMOUR
2nd Assistant Editor	VALENTINA GIAMBANCO
Editing Jobfit	IAN MACBETH
Supervising Sound Editor	SUE BAKER
Dialogue Editor	COLIN RITCHIE
2nd Dialogue Editor	JUPITER SEN
Foley Editor	ANDREW GLEN
Assistant Sound Editor	DEREK LOMAS
Assistant Dialogue Editor	SARAH RAINS
Foley Artists	JACK STEW
	DIANNE GREAVES
Dubbing Mixer	PETER MAXWELL
Assistant Dubbing Mixer	MICK BOGGIS
Music Researcher	JOHN LUNN

Wardrobe Supervisor	JOHN SCOTT
Assistant to Costume Designer	DEBBIE SCOTT
Wardrobe Assistants	NIGEL EGERTON
	ALISON WYLDECK
Wardrobe Runner	ODILON ROCHA
Hairdresser	FRANCESCA CROWDER
Make-up/Hair Assistants	TRACEY LEE
	MELISSA LACKERSTEEN
Make-up/Hair PA	JULIA FETTERMAN
Set Decorator	ANNA PINNOCK
Assistant Art Director	PHIL ROBINSON
Flowers by	SIMON J. LYCETT
Property Master	BARRY WILKINSON
Storeman	CHARLIE IXER
Dressing Props	PETER WALLIS
	PAUL CHEESMAN
	JAMIE WILKINSON
Chargehand Standby Propman	SIMON WILKINSON
Standby Propman	GARY IXER
Construction	DAVE ALLEN
Standby Carpenter	TOMMY WESTBROOK
Standby Stagehand	BRIAN MITCHELL
Standby Rigger	CON MURPHY
Standby Painter	KEN HAWKEY
Gaffer	TERRY EDLAND
Best Boy	WAYNE LEACH
Rigging Gaffer	VINCE CLARKE
Electricians	PAUL KEMP
	DARREN GATTRELL
Generator Operator	JIMMY COWARD
Assistants to Mr Kenworthy	KAY ROBINSON
	WENDY DADE
Assistant to Mr Curtis	CHARLOTTE LAUGHTON
Production Runner	JUSTIN DAVIES
Floor Runner	CHRISTIAN JAMES
Casting Assistant	SARAH BEARDSALL
Aristocracy Co-ordinator	AMBER RUDD
Sign Language Consultants	WENDY EBSWORTH
	VICKI GEE DARE
SFX Supervisor	IAN WINGROVE
Stunt Co-ordinator	WAYNE MICHAELS
Stunt Drivers	WENDY LEACH
	CLIVE CURTIS
Publicist	ELAINE ROBERTSON
Stills Photographer	STEPHEN MORLEY
Stand-Ins	STEVEN RICARDS
	LEAH FOLEY
	JOHN LOCKE
Unit Nurse	ROSIE BEDFORD-STRADLING
Unit Drivers	MICK BEAVEN
	ENYONAM MORTTY
	JED BRAY
	ROY CLARKE
Location Transport	D & D TRANSPORT
	LOCATION FACILITIES
Camera Truck Driver	JOHN OTT
Wardrobe Bus Driver	NICK HEATHER
Make-up/Hair Bus Driver	JOHN SQUIRES
Standby Props Driver	TOM INNES
Standby Construction Driver	TED DEBRERA
Grip Truck Driver	MARTIN O'CONNOR
Props Runaround Driver	TERRY STINSON
Trailers	DAVE JONES
Crowd Coaches/Crew Mini-Buses	HILLS OF HERSHAM
Mini-Bus Drivers	TONY MARSHALL
	DAVID CARR

Catering by	BUSTERS ON LOCATION
Caterers	STEVE PASMORE
	GEORGE SCHEMBRI
	RUBY RAWLINS
	NATASHA HUDSON
	JON SYMONDS
	CLARE GREENWOOD

FOR WORKING TITLE

Production Executives	JANE FRAZER
	DEBORAH HARDING
Legal & Business Affairs	CAROLINE SOUTHEY
	ANGELA MORRISON
Financial Controller	ANDY MAYSON
Head of Development	DEBRA HAYWARD
Assistants to Executive Producers	JULIETTE DOW
	NATASCHA WHARTON

PR Consultants	DENNIS DAVIDSON ASSOC. LIMITED
Camera & Lenses by	J. DUNTON & COMPANY LIMITED
Originated on	EASTMAN COLOUR FILM FROM KODAK
Colour by	METROCOLOR LONDON LIMITED
Lighting Eqipment Supplied by	LEE LIGHTING LIMITED
Grip Equipment	J. DUNTON & COMPANY LIMITED
Costumiers	BERMANS ANGELS
Production Facilities	SHEPPERTON STUDIOS
Post Production Facilities & Sound Re-recording	
	DE LANE LEA SOUND CENTRE
Big Cheese	MICHAEL KUHN
Title Design	CHRIS ALLIES
Motion Control Camera	PETER TYLER
Opticals & Subtitling	CAPITAL FX LIMITED
Rostrum Camera	FRAMELINE
Stills Processing	BLOW UP PHOTOGRAPHERS
Completion Guaranty Provided by	
	INTERNATIONAL FILM GUARANTORS, INC.
Insurance	RHH/ALBERT G. RUBEN
	KEVIN O'SHEA

THE POEM 'FUNERAL BLUES: STOP ALL THE CLOCKS, CUT OFF THE
TELEPHONE...' BY W.H. AUDEN
FROM THE BOOK *ANOTHER TIME* BY W.H. AUDEN
USED BY KIND PERMISSION OF CURTIS BROWN, LTD.
COPYRIGHT © 1940 BY W.H. AUDEN, RENEWED
ALL RIGHTS RESERVED

EXTRACT FROM **'MIND GAMES'**
WRITTEN BY JOHN LENNON
COURTESY OF BMG MUSIC PUBLISHING LTD.

MUSIC RECORDED & MIXED BY DICK LEWZEY AT CTS & LANSDOWNE RECORDING STUDIOS LIMITED IN LONDON, ENGLAND.

Orchestrator, Conductor & Arranger of Source Music
NEIL RICHARDSON
Rock & Roll Band (Wedding One) DAVID WRIGHT, RAY UREN
GORDON BLACKWELL, RON GRIFFITHS
Swing Band (Wedding Two) RICHARD ALLEN, MARK JAMES
JASON BRUER, SIMON WALLACE, JASON McDERMID
BRYN BURROWS, PAULETTE IVORY

'BUT NOT FOR ME'
PERFORMED BY ELTON JOHN   PRODUCED BY STEVE LINDSEY WRITTEN BY
GEORGE GERSHWIN & IRA GERSHWIN
PUBLISHED BY WARNER CHAPPELL MUSIC LTD
(P) 1993 WILLIAM A. BONG LTD

'CHAPEL OF LOVE'
PERFORMED BY ELTON JOHN   PRODUCED BY STEVE LINDSEY
WRITTEN BY PHIL SPECTOR, JEFF BARRY & ELLIE GREENWICH
PUBLISHED BY MOTHER BERTHA MUSIC, INC.
BY ARRANGEMENT WITH ABKCO MUSIC, INC. & CARLIN MUSIC
CORPORATION BY ARRANGEMENT WITH TRIO MUSIC, INC.
(P) 1993 WILLIAM A. BONG LTD

ELTON JOHN APPEARS COURTESY OF PHONOGRAM LTD
& MCA RECORDS, INC.

'BUT NOT FOR ME' & 'CHAPEL OF LOVE' RECORDED AT OCEAN WAY
RECORDING STUDIOS. LOS ANGELES & METROPOLIS, LONDON

'STAND BY YOUR MAN'
WRITTEN BY TAMMY WYNETTE & BILLY SHERRILL
PUBLISHED BY EMI MUSIC (UK) LTD

'CAN'T SMILE WITHOUT YOU'
WRITTEN BY ARNOLD/MARTIN/MORROW
PUBLISHED BY POLYGRAM MUSIC PUBLISHING LTD

'CROCODILE ROCK'
WRITTEN BY JOHN/TAUPIN
PUBLISHED BY POLYGRAM MUSIC PUBLISHING LTD

'I WILL SURVIVE'
WRITTEN BY PERREN/FEKARIS
PUBLISHED BY POLYGRAM INTERNATIONAL PUBLISHING INC.

'WALKING BACK TO HAPPINESS'
WRITTEN BY SCHROEDER/HAWKER
PUBLISHED BY POLYGRAM MUSIC PUBLISHING LTD

'LOVE IS ALL AROUND'
WRITTEN BY PRESLEY   PUBLISHED BY POLYGRAM MUSIC PUBLISHING LTD

'SMOKE GETS IN YOUR EYES'
WRITTEN BY KERN/HARBACK
PUBLISHED BY POLYGRAM INTERNATIONAL PUBLISHING INC.

'GONNA GET ALONG WITHOUT YOU NOW'
WRITTEN BY KELLEN
PUBLISHED BY POLYGRAM INTERNATIONAL PUBLISHING INC.

'DANCE FOR NORMAN'
COMPOSED & PERFORMED BY IRA NEWBORN
PUBLISHED BY NEWBORN MUSIC PUBLISHING, CO

'THE DASHING WHITE SERGEANT'
TRADITIONAL ARRANGED BY BILL BLACK
PERFORMED BY BILL BLACK   PUBLISHED BY SPRINGTHYME MUSIC
(P) 1992 SPRINGTHYME RECORDS

Bridalgowns provided by **BERKERTEX BRIDES**

Thanks to **TONI GARD** for Assistance with
Ms MacDowell's wardrobe

China & Linen by
RAYNERS CATERING & EQUIPMENT HIRE

Hair Products by **L'OREAL**

With thanks to **STEWART TILL   JANE MOORE
KATHRYN SMITH   MARK WOLFE   JOHN FISHLOCK
JOHN REID   CLIVE BANKS   ALISON O'BRIEN
CLAIRE CHRISTIE   COMPLETE EVENTS
LOUIS VUITTON   OAKTREE FUNERAL SERVICES
THURROCK COUNCIL   HERALD & HEART HATS
JIM HENSON PRODUCTIONS**

FILMED ENTIRELY ON LOCATION IN
LONDON AND THE HOME COUNTIES OF ENGLAND